A MINISTER
EVERYONE WOULD RESPECT
A STUDY OF 2 CORINTHIANS 8–13

BIBLE STUDY GUIDE

From the Bible-teaching ministry of

Charles R. Swindoll

INSIGHT FOR LIVING

Charles R. Swindoll is a graduate of Dallas Theological Seminary and has served in pastorates since 1963, including churches in Texas, New England, and California. Since 1971 he has served as senior pastor of the First Evangelical Free Church of Fullerton, California. Chuck's radio program, "Insight for Living," began in 1979. In addition to his church and radio ministries, Chuck has authored numerous books and booklets on a variety of subjects.

Based on the outlines and transcripts of Chuck's sermons, the study guide text is coauthored by Ken Gire, a graduate of Texas Christian University and Dallas Theological Seminary. The Living Insights are written by Bill Butterworth, a graduate of Florida Bible College, Dallas Theological Seminary, and Florida Atlantic University.

Editor in Chief:
Cynthia Swindoll

Coauthor of Text:
Ken Gire

Author of Living Insights:
Bill Butterworth

Assistant Editor:
Karene Wells

Editorial Assistant:
Glenda Schlata

Copy Manager:
Jac La Tour

Copyediting Supervisor:
Marty Anderson

Copy Editor:
Connie Laser

Director, Communications Division:
Carla Beck

Project Manager:
Alene Cooper

Project Supervisor:
Cassandra Clark

Art Director:
Don Pierce

Designer:
Gary Lett

Typographer:
Bob Haskins

Print Production Manager:
Deedee Snyder

Unless otherwise identified, all Scripture references are from the New American Standard Bible, © The Lockman Foundation 1960, 1962, 1963, 1968, 1971, 1972, 1973, 1975, 1977. Used by permission.

An effort has been made to locate sources and obtain permission where necessary for the quotations used in this book. In the event of any unintentional omission, a modification will gladly be incorporated in future printings.

ISBN 0-8499-8404-1
Printed in the United States of America.

COVER PHOTOGRAPH: Owen Riss

CONTENTS

*This message was not a part of the original series but is compatible with it.

A MINISTER EVERYONE WOULD RESPECT
A STUDY OF 2 CORINTHIANS 8–13

T he second letter Paul wrote to the Corinthians is his most autobiographical. From these pages we not only learn a great deal about the qualities of his ministry, we discover the man himself. And what a man he was . . . a minister everyone respected.

In the final six chapters of this letter, Paul unveils many things about his life that are mentioned nowhere else in Scripture. Among these are his convictions regarding financial generosity, the criticism he lived with and hardships he endured, his struggle with a "thorn in the flesh," and even his tender affection for fellow Christians. We want to examine each one carefully. But more importantly, let's commit ourselves to cultivating a similar philosophy of life, because such models are rare today!

I commend you for your diligence to stay with me through the latter half of Second Corinthians. Like me, you are probably realizing how far the church in general and God's people in particular have drifted from the first-century pattern. My prayer is that God will enable us to believe what we discover in His Word and then use what we learn to make a difference in a day like ours when many in ministry have lost their way . . . and others' respect.

Chuck Swindoll

Chuck Swindoll

PUTTING TRUTH INTO ACTION

Knowledge apart from application falls short of God's desire for His children. He wants us to apply what we learn so that we will change and grow. This study guide was prepared with these goals in mind. As you go through the following pages, we hope your desire to discover biblical truth will grow as your understanding of God's Word increases, and that you will be encouraged to apply what you've learned.

To assist you in your study, we've included a section called **Living Insights** at the end of each lesson. These exercises will challenge you to study further and to think of specific ways to put your discoveries into action.

There are many ways to use this guide—in personal devotions, group studies, discussions with friends and family, and Sunday school classes. And, of course, it's an ideal study aid when you're listening to its corresponding "Insight for Living" radio series.

To benefit most from this study guide, we would encourage you to consider it a spiritual journal. That's why we've included space in the **Living Insights** for recording your thoughts and discoveries. We hope you'll return to those sections often for review and encouragement as you continue to grow in your walk with Christ.

Ken Gire
Coauthor of Text

Bill Butterworth
Author of Living Insights

A MINISTER
EVERYONE WOULD RESPECT

A STUDY OF 2 CORINTHIANS 8–13

Chapter 1

MAKING GOOD SENSE WITH OUR DOLLARS

2 Corinthians 8:1–9

A story is told about a man who, after twenty years of marriage, decided to divorce his wife. In preparing for the financial settlement, he began to rummage through his old checks.

One canceled check after another stirred up memories of a long-forgotten past: the check to the hotel where he and his wife had spent their honeymoon, the check for their first car, the check for the hospital bill for their daughter's birth, the check for the $2,000 down payment on their first home.

Finally, he could stand it no longer. He pushed the checks aside, reached for the telephone, and called his wife. Telling her they had invested too much in each other to throw it all away, he asked her to start over with him in a fresh beginning.

Our own checkbook also tells the story of our life—our values and our lifestyle. And more than almost anything else, that checkbook reveals our true walk with God. Because our checkbook announces what our treasures are.

Jesus said a lot about treasure while He was on earth. In fact, one third of His parables address the subject of stewardship. He spoke extensively about it, not because He was a fund-raiser, but because He knew that "where your treasure is, there will your heart be also" (Matt. 6:21).

Clarification of Major Scriptures on Giving

Stewardship is a key principle in Scripture—stewardship of our time, our talents, and our treasures. Regarding the last, there are

1

four primary passages for us to consider, particularly in regard to investing those treasures in ministry.

1 Corinthians 9

This passage provides the justification for giving.

> If we sowed spiritual things in you, is it too much if we should reap material things from you? . . . Do you not know that those who perform sacred services eat the food of the temple, and those who attend regularly to the altar have their share with the altar? So also the Lord directed those who proclaim the gospel to get their living from the gospel. (vv. 11, 13–14)

Even though remuneration for the ministry is specifically sanctioned by God, Paul chose not to receive money for his spiritual labor (vv. 12, 15–18; Acts 20:33–35).

1 Corinthians 16

This passage provides the instructions for giving.

> Now concerning the collection for the saints, as I directed the churches of Galatia, so do you also. On the first day of every week let each one of you put aside and save, as he may prosper, that no collections be made when I come. (vv. 1–2)

For all who wonder about procedure, these two verses supply us with a good checklist for giving.

1. Systematically—"on the first day of every week"

2. Individually—"let each one of you"

3. Consistently—"put aside and save"

4. Proportionately—"as he may prosper"

5. Privately—"no collections be made when I come"

In these verses we see no pressure, no announcement, no public attention, and no manipulative techniques. How different from today.

2 Corinthians 8

This passage, which will be the focus of today's lesson, shows us two illustrations of giving: first, the Macedonians (vv. 1–3); and second, Jesus Christ (v. 9).

2 Corinthians 9

This passage reveals the application of giving.

> "He scattered abroad, he gave to the poor,
> His righteousness abides forever." (v. 9)

Giving, like the rest of the Christian life, is not to be done out of rote obedience to law or out of pressure from others. It is a matter of the heart and should, ideally, be done with the most free and willing of attitudes.

Explanation of Paul's Remarks on Giving

The historical context behind chapters 8 and 9 is the great financial need within the mother church at Jerusalem.[1] Recognizing that need, the churches in Macedonia rallied to the occasion.[2]

An Illustration of the Macedonians

> Now, brethren, we wish to make known to you the grace of God which has been given in the churches of Macedonia, that in a great ordeal of affliction their abundance of joy and their deep poverty overflowed in the wealth of their liberality. (8:1–2)

Generally, we would assume that an outpouring of generosity would come from churches that were wealthy and could afford a gracious, philanthropic gesture. But such was not the case with the Macedonian churches. They were physically afflicted and financially depleted.[3] The Romans had taken possession of all their silver and

---

1. "The preaching of the Apostles on the day of Pentecost (May 26, A.D. 30) and on subsequent days had been attended by the conversion of thousands of souls (see Acts 2:41, 4:4). The material cost to the majority of this great number must have been immense. Coming as they did from the background of Jewish fervour and exclusivism, it needs no demonstration that they must have become, in consequence of their conversion, the victims of social and economic ostracism, ecclesiastical excommunication, and national disinheritance. Their business enterprises must in most cases have collapsed in ruins and family bonds been heart-breakingly severed." Philip Edgcumbe Hughes, *Paul's Second Epistle to the Corinthians* (Grand Rapids, Mich.: William B. Eerdmans Publishing Co., 1962), p. 284.

2. The churches in Macedonia are probably the ones Paul founded at Philippi, Thessalonica, and Berea (Acts 16:11–17:13).

3. "In addition to being extremely poor, the Macedonian Christians had recently been subjected to considerable persecution which had tested their faith." R. V. G. Tasker, *The Second Epistle of Paul to the Corinthians* (Grand Rapids, Mich.: William B. Eerdmans Publishing Co., 1958), p. 111. See 1 Thessalonians 1:6–7 and Acts 17:1–9 for references to the persecution of the Macedonians and Paul.

gold mines, taxed the copper and iron smelting, canceled the right to cut trees for ship and home building, and had fought several wars on Macedonian soil.

Yet in spite of their "great ordeal of affliction," they gave with an "abundance of joy." And in spite of "their deep poverty," they "overflowed in the wealth of their liberality." Verse 3 adds still another dimension.

> For I testify that according to their ability, and beyond
> their ability they gave of their own accord. (v. 3)

They gave voluntarily, "of their own *accord*" (emphasis added). This word is used only here and in verse 17 in all the New Testament. The Macedonians gave spontaneously, with no prompting or pressure from Paul. In fact, they even pleaded with Paul and Titus to take their money. Paul notes in verse 4 that they were

> begging us with much entreaty for the favor of partici-
> pation in the support of the saints.

What is it that prompts such excitement and enthusiastic participation in meeting a need that calls for such sacrifice? The answer is found in the word *favor.* The original Greek term means "grace," the same word used in verse 1. The Macedonians didn't see helping needy believers as an obligation but a privilege. This is grace-giving at its finest. And the following verse shows the soil from which this type of gracious giving originates.

> They first gave themselves to the Lord and to us by
> the will of God. (v. 5b)

When you give yourself totally to the Lord, giving your time, talents, or treasures is part and parcel of that commitment. You don't have to be convinced or manipulated or coerced. You give freely, with an open hand and an open heart. And if you find yourself giving with a tight fist, the problem is probably deeper than your wallet.

A Reminder to the Corinthians

Having given the example of the Macedonians, Paul now turns his attention to the original generosity of the Corinthians and their need to complete a project they had begun.

> Consequently we urged Titus that as he had previously
> made a beginning, so he would also complete in you
> this gracious work as well. (v. 6)

Unlike the Macedonians, who were being ground under the heel of a cruel Roman boot, the Corinthians were flourishing. They had the ability to complete the work they had started a year earlier. Regarding this "gracious work," Paul comments:

> But just as you abound in everything, in faith and utterance and knowledge and in all earnestness and in the love we inspired in you, see that you abound in this gracious work also. (v. 7)

First, the apostle reminds the church how they abound in so many blessings. Second, he tells them they are lacking in balance, because the abounding didn't carry over to their giving.

Think about yourself for a minute. How balanced is your life? Are you just as committed in your giving as you are to Bible study or to prayer or to worship? If the margins of your Bible are crowded with spiritual notes but your checkbook is crowded only with entries like Sears, Penney's, Visa, and American Express, chances are your life is out of balance.

Such a reminder could have been misconstrued by the Corinthians. But Paul is quick to keep that from happening.

> I am not speaking this as a command, but as proving through the earnestness of others the sincerity of your love also. (v. 8)

Paul wasn't berating the church by barking orders. He was appealing to them, through the example of the Macedonians, to rekindle the dormant embers of their love. And to do this, he fans the fire with a picture of Jesus.

The Example of Christ

No better example of gracious giving exists than the life of Christ.

> For you know the grace of our Lord Jesus Christ, that though He was rich, yet for your sake He became poor, that you through His poverty might become rich. (v. 9)

There's the word *grace* again.[4] On the basis of grace Paul makes his appeal. Notice the subtle contrast. Though the Macedonians were poor, they gave like they were rich. Though Jesus was rich, he lived like He was poor. Both provide a beautiful illustration for giving. Jesus was the wealthiest person in all the universe, for it was all His, deeded to Him by the Father. Yet He left it behind.

---

4. This is the fifth time a form of *grace* has been used in this passage (*grace*, v. 1; *favor*, v. 4; *gracious*, v. 6; *gracious*, v. 7; *grace*, v. 9). The subtle implication is that our giving should come from a context of grace—not guilt.

Although He existed in the form of God, [He] did not regard equality with God a thing to be grasped, but emptied Himself, taking the form of a bond-servant, and being made in the likeness of men. And being found in appearance as a man, He humbled Himself by becoming obedient to the point of death, even death on a cross. (Phil. 2:6–8)

Application of Biblical Truth on Giving

As we come to the end of our study today, a couple of thoughts rise to the surface.

First: *Claiming God's grace without receiving God's Son is an impossibility.* Any person who claims to live by grace without a relationship with Jesus is mistaken.

Second: *Walking in grace without giving our treasure is incomplete.* If we give ourselves totally to God, that will affect how we give to others.

Let's get painfully personal for a moment. If you were to rummage through your checks, as the man at the beginning of our lesson did, what spiritual values would be revealed? If a biographer were trying to piece together a composite of your life from your checks, what picture would emerge? Would you look like a materialist? A glutton? An egoist? Or would you look like Jesus, who though He was rich, yet for the sake of others became poor?

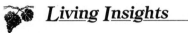 *Living Insights* STUDY ONE

As we embark on another voyage of biblical discovery, it would be wise to get our bearings by looking at where we've been and where we're going.

- If you're just beginning your study of 2 Corinthians, use this time to skim over the first seven chapters to find out what Paul has already covered. And even if you've studied these chapters in our previous study guide, the review will be helpful. In the space provided jot down any discoveries you make.

My Thoughts on 2 Corinthians

_____

_____

_____

Take out your checkbook for a minute. In the space below duplicate your check register for the past month. If you need additional space, continue your entries on a separate piece of paper.

Check Number	Description of Transaction	Payment	Balance

Imagine for a moment that you are a biographer doing research on the person who wrote the checks. And let's say that the check register is all the data you have to evaluate that person's life. From the checkbook, what kind of composite picture could you draw about that person's life and values? Where would you say that person's treasure lies?

Chapter 2

FANNING THE FINANCIAL FIRE

2 Corinthians 8:10-24

I n our last lesson, we were introduced to an incredible body of Christians: the Macedonian church. Despite poverty and affliction, they gave generously to the needy church in Jerusalem. Faithfully they sent their relief checks and care packages, stoking the fire of generosity that burned in their hearts.

The Corinthian church had likewise begun a Jerusalem-Aid project, but after their initial spark of enthusiasm, their good intentions sputtered under the routine of daily life.

So Paul took up his pen and stirred the dying embers, encouraging the Corinthians to complete the work they had started the year before. In doing so, the apostle urged them to examine carefully their hearts as well as their finances. As we study his words, let's examine our hearts too, allowing Paul to fan the financial fire until it blazes freely within us.

Four Words That Free Us Financially

Whatever the state of your finances, four simple words will give you financial freedom: God owns it all. He owns it *all*. That principle underlies all of Scripture.

"Whatever is under the whole heaven is Mine."
(Job 41:11)

"All the earth is Mine." (Exod. 19:5)

The earth is the Lord's, and everything in it,
the world, and all who live in it. (Ps. 24:1, NIV)

You are not your own. (1 Cor. 6:19)

You were bought with a price. (1 Cor. 7:23)

We have brought nothing into the world, so we cannot take anything out of it either. (1 Tim. 6:7)

We are born into this world with empty hands, and we leave with empty pockets. God owns it all. Listen to what one prominent financial counselor says on that subject.

Very few Christians would argue with the principle that God owns it all, and yet if we follow that principle to its natural conclusion, there are three revolutionary implications. First of all, God has the right to whatever He wants whenever He wants it. It is all His, because an owner has *rights*, and I, as a steward, have only *responsibilities*. . . .

If I really believe that God owns it all then when I lose any possession, for whatever reason, my emotions may cry out, but my mind and spirit have not the slightest question as to the right of God to take whatever He wants whenever He wants it. Really believing this also frees me to give generously of God's resources to God's purposes and His people. All that I have belongs to Him.

The second implication of God's owning it all is that not only is my giving decision a spiritual decision, but *every* spending decision is a spiritual decision. . . . As a steward, I have a great deal of latitude, but I am still responsible to the Owner. Some day I will give an accounting of how I used His property.

The third implication of the truth that God owns it all is that you can't fake stewardship. Your checkbook reveals all that you really believe about stewardship . . . your goals, priorities, convictions, relationships, and even the use of your time. A person who has been a Christian for even a short while can fake prayer, Bible study, evangelism, going to church, and so on, but he can't fake what his checkbook reveals.[1]

Once we come to terms with that basic principle—God owns it all—we will be open to handling our finances God's way. This isn't easy for us today, nor was it easy for the Corinthians.

Putting Those Words to the Test Back Then

One year after the Corinthian church had first agreed to contribute to the church in Jerusalem, their contributions had dwindled to nothing. Paul seeks to motivate them by offering three incentives, cautioning them on four hindrances, and reminding them of two principles.

1. Ron Blue, *Master Your Money* (Nashville, Tenn.: Thomas Nelson Publishers, 1986), pp. 19–20. Used by permission.

Three Incentives

By way of review, we find these incentives for giving in 2 Corinthians 8:7–9.

First: *Stop and consider the blessings of God.* The Corinthians abounded "in everything" (v. 7). They had faith, good teaching, knowledge, earnestness, and love. We can also gather that they were probably quite well-off. That's why Paul tells them to count their blessings (see also Ps. 103).

Second: *Listen to the testimony of others* (2 Cor. 8:8). "Others" here refers to the Macedonians, a church that gave abundantly in spite of knowing much hardship and little material wealth.

Third: *Look at the example of Christ* (v. 9). As we learned in our last lesson, Jesus is our perfect model of giving.

The next time you're reluctant to give, count your blessings, call to mind a few testimonies of those who have given faithfully, and consider Christ's gift to you. You'll find your grip a little looser, and your worries a little less significant.

Four Hindrances

Why then do we still tend to hold back? Why are we reluctant to be generous with our money? Paul presents four hindrances that surfaced in the Corinthians' lives, problems we all can identify with. The first is *procrastination*.

> And I give my opinion in this matter, for this is to your advantage, who were the first to begin a year ago not only to do this, but also to desire to do it. But now finish doing it also. (vv. 10–11a)

Webster says to *procrastinate* is to put off intentionally and habitually the doing of something that should be done.[2] Procrastination has also been called the art of keeping up with yesterday. The procrastinator's favorite word? Tomorrow. "Tomorrow I'll get organized . . . tomorrow I'll go on a diet . . . tomorrow I'll start giving to the poor." The Corinthians had fallen into that trap, but Paul says no, do it now. Notice verse 11: "Now finish doing it." Don't think about it; do it. Now.

A close kin to procrastination is *hesitation,* the second hindrance. Hesitation says, "I'm just not ready." Take a look at Paul's response to that excuse.

---

2. *Webster's Ninth New Collegiate Dictionary,* see "procrastinate."

Just as there was the readiness to desire it, so there may be also the completion of it by your ability. For if the readiness is present, it is acceptable according to what a man has, not according to what he does not have. (vv. 11b–12)

Readiness means "eagerness, motivation, enthusiasm, getting excited about," which is the opposite of hesitation. Paul says to the Corinthians, "If you have readiness, you can do it. You can complete the project, even if you don't think you have the resources."

Look again at verse 12, for here we find a third hindrance: *overreaction.*

For if the readiness is present, it is acceptable according to what a man has, not according to what he does not have.

This verse ties in with the last three words of verse 11—"by your ability." The person who overreacts says, "Because I'm not able to give as much as someone else, I'm not going to give anything at all." The trouble with that kind of thinking is that someone else will always make more money than we will and therefore give more.

Paul reminds us that God assesses our monetary gifts not by the actual amount given but by comparing it with our total financial resources. Remember the story of the poor widow in Mark 12? She is a beautiful illustration of this point.

[Jesus] sat down opposite the treasury, and began observing how the multitude were putting money into the treasury; and many rich people were putting in large sums. And a poor widow came and put in two small copper coins, which amount to a cent.[3] And calling His disciples to Him, He said to them, "Truly I say to you, this poor widow put in more than all the contributors to the treasury; for they all put in out of their surplus, but she, out of her poverty, put in all she owned, all she had to live on." (vv. 41–44)

Our giving is acceptable to God according to what we have, not according to what we don't have. The widow had little, but she gave it all, and God honored her.

The fourth hindrance can be called *exception.* This hindrance says, "Since others have it easier financially than I do, I am not responsible. I'm an exception."

3. This represented 1/64 of a denarius.

For this is not for the ease of others and for your affliction, but by way of equality—at this present time your abundance being a supply for their want, that their abundance also may become a supply for your want, that there may be equality; as it is written, "He who gathered much did not have too much, and he who gathered little had no lack."[4] (2 Cor. 8:13–15)

Paul is saying that God, the great equalizer, has a way of balancing out our provisions. Right now, the church in Jerusalem needs assistance from the Corinthians, but later the burden may shift and the Corinthians may be the ones in need.

Procrastination, hesitation, overreaction, exception—these hindrances relate to the giver. Paul concludes this chapter by focusing on the recipient of the funds.

Two Principles

The first principle deals with the people involved in a financial project, the second with the process of administration.

Principle number one: *Only qualified people should handle financial matters.*

But thanks be to God, who puts the same earnestness on your behalf in the heart of Titus. For he not only accepted our appeal, but being himself very earnest, he has gone to you of his own accord. And we have sent along with him the brother whose fame in the things of the gospel has spread through all the churches; and not only this, but he has also been appointed by the churches to travel with us in this gracious work, which is being administered by us for the glory of the Lord Himself, and to show our readiness. . . . And we have sent with them our brother, whom we have often tested and found diligent in many things. . . . As for Titus, he is my partner and fellow worker among you; as for our brethren, they are messengers of the churches, a glory to Christ. (vv. 16–19, 22a, 23)

Paul appointed three men—Titus and two unnamed "brothers" —to work in this area. Did you see their list of credentials? Earnestness (v. 16); a willing heart (v. 17); appointed by the churches (v. 19); diligent (v. 22); a partner and fellow worker (v. 23); and a glory to Christ (v. 23).

4. Paul is quoting from Exodus 16:18, which tells how the Israelites gathered the manna from heaven: "Every man gathered as much as he should eat."

Principle number two: *Money matters should be administered honestly and openly.*

> [This project] is being administered by us for the glory of the Lord Himself, and to show our readiness, taking precaution that no one should discredit us in our administration of this generous gift; for we have regard for what is honorable, not only in the sight of the Lord, but also in the sight of men. (vv. 19b–21)

Why must we be so cautious? First, God is watching how we spend His money. And second, we are accountable not only to Him but to others as well. When people give their money to churches, ministries, and charities, they trust that their money will be used wisely and carefully. That trust must be guarded, for a ministry can't operate without it.

Paul closes by saying, in essence, "Get the job done."

> Therefore openly before the churches show them the proof of your love and of our reason for boasting about you. (v. 24)

Passing the Test Today

To add fuel to the flame that hopefully has ignited in your heart, take these concluding moments to consider how Paul's words apply to you personally. How would you respond to these five questions?

1. Do I really believe God owns it all?

2. Have I recently considered God's blessings?

3. Am I currently refusing to hide behind excuses?

4. Can I honestly say I'm convinced of the integrity of the ministry I support?

5. Will I diligently begin to dethrone money from my life?

Living Insights   STUDY ONE

Four words that free us financially: God owns it all. This passage in chapter 8 speaks succinctly to that issue. Let's look at it more closely.

• One way to glean greater meaning out of a text is to rewrite that text in your own words. This allows you to heighten the meanings

14

and emotions that penetrate the passage. Begin a paraphrase of chapter 8 at verse 10. Continue as far as you can through the chapter in the time available to you. Think especially of how Paul's words apply to you personally.

My Paraphrase

_____

_____

_____

_____

_____

_____

_____

_____

_____

_____

_____

_____

_____

_____

_____

_____

_____

_____

_____

_____

_____

_____

Since our lesson concluded with five thought-provoking questions, it would be wise to take the time to consider them in more depth. As you ponder each question, write out your thoughts in the space provided.

- Do I really believe God owns it all?

  _____

  _____

  _____

- Have I recently considered God's blessings?

  _____

  _____

  _____

- Am I currently refusing to hide behind excuses?

  _____

  _____

  _____

- Can I honestly say I'm convinced of the integrity of the ministry I support?

  _____

  _____

  _____

- Will I diligently begin to dethrone money from my life?

  _____

  _____

  _____

Chapter 3

THE TRIP TO BOUNTIFUL GIVING

2 Corinthians 9:1–6

T he setting is the lobby of the Peabody Hotel, Orlando, Florida. The theme song is John Philip Sousa's "Stars and Stripes Forever." The stage is a strip of red carpeting across the main floor, and the performers are a flock of web-footed, high-stepping, orange-billed ducks. They muster their troops at the fountain, then march out in a straight line to the delighted applause of hotel guests, twice a day. It's the Peabody's Parade of Ducks.

How in the world do you get a flock of ducks to step in time across a hotel lobby? Twice a day, no less?

The answer is waiting backstage—food. Those ducks don't care about performing. They aren't concentrating on their waddling or on the red carpet or even on the applause. Their minds are on what's behind the curtain. They know waddling across that lobby is the only way they're going to get fed, so they're willing to waddle. But waddling to applause isn't really where their hearts are.

There's an analogy to be drawn between those marching ducks and people today who need to get a big job done.

The Essential Ingredients of Accomplishment

Who hasn't struggled with ways to approach a job? We are always looking for secrets of accomplishment. In this lesson we'll see that no matter how big the task, there are always four essential ingredients for achieving a goal.

First: *There must be active participants.* When you're facing a monumental task, it's no time to don your Lone Ranger mask. You can't always do it alone. You've got to call out the troops—people who will take an active part to help you.

Second: *There must be clear objectives.* Without the red carpet, the Peabody ducks wouldn't know where to waddle. They'd be swimming in the fountain or quacking around the lobby or taking the escalator up to the mezzanine. That red carpet keeps them marching in a straight line right across that floor and behind the curtain to their goal—lunch. Like the ducks, you have to know where you're going if you're going to get a job done.

Third: *There must be strong enthusiasm.* This is what puts the prance in the march of the ducks. It puts the oil on the gears, the fun in the job. Any task will fall flat if it lacks enthusiasm.

Fourth: *There must be the promise of reward.* The ducks had plenty of inner incentive for strutting across that hotel lobby—hungry tummies and the smell of duck food. Tangible rewards fuel the fire of determination and keep our bills headed backstage. But behind that curtain, apart from the food, there was something else that was very important . . . a person who loved ducks. Somebody who had thought the program through, organized the details, and set up the stage. Some projects require a designated leader like that. Even the Exodus wasn't coordinated by committee; God appointed Moses to lead the charge. And God didn't build a wall around Jerusalem by popular vote; He sent a leader named Nehemiah to get the job done.

People are willing to do almost anything if they really believe in the task. John Gardner said, "The best-kept secret in America today is that people would rather work hard for something they believe in than enjoy a pampered idleness."[1] We will work for less with greater enthusiasm if we really believe in the project. We will pass up a job that pays more if it requires us to do something we really don't believe in. It happens all the time.

Back in the first century, there was a big job to be done. The leader behind it all was a man named Paul, who wrote a few letters to those who could make it happen—the Corinthians, members of a fine, gifted, well-taught, thriving church. The job? To collect an offering for the church in Jerusalem, a little struggling church on the other side of the Mediterranean that was against the wall financially.

Paul dedicates no less than two entire chapters to that project in this second letter to the Corinthians. And as we work our way through those chapters, we'll find that all four of those ingredients for accomplishment are in place.

The Unstated Equation of Generosity

In his appeal to the Corinthians, Paul sets up an unstated equation of generosity.

---

1. John W. Gardner, as quoted in *Bringing Out the Best in People,* by Alan Loy McGinnis (Minneapolis, Minn.: Augsburg Publishing House, 1985), p. 55.

Implied

In the first verse of 2 Corinthians 9, Paul spends a rare moment backpedaling.

> For it is superfluous for me to write to you about this ministry to the saints.

The word *superfluous* means "unnecessary, extra, nonessential." It's as if Paul knows that the ingredients for accomplishing the task are already in place. He's talked to the Corinthians before about giving, and some of them have already begun to respond. So here he's enjoying the kind of satisfaction that comes from knowing you're on the right track. He's got the equation set up, and he knows it's going to work. That implied equation?

> (The right people + the right goal) x (direction + enthusiasm) = accomplishment.

In other words, when the right people are pursuing the right goal with enough direction and enthusiasm, they will give more than enough!

Paul had all the elements of the equation in place. But the key to any major project is having the right leadership. There is no way to underestimate the value of a good leader.

More of us than we know hold the power of leadership in our hands. Are you leading anyone? If you're a mother, you are. If you're a father, you are. You may be a leader in your neighborhood or at your job. Leadership can happen without a vote, without any kind of official notification.

Be careful with the leadership you find in your life. Remember— another side of Paul's equation is that leadership equals influence.

Explained

In verses 2–5, Paul bounces back and forth between talking about the Corinthians and talking about himself. It's an interchange of thoughts between the participants and the leader. Watch how Paul goes about inspiring the Corinthians to an even greater generosity.

> For I know your readiness, of which I boast about you to the Macedonians, namely, that Achaia has been prepared since last year, and your zeal has stirred up most of them. (v. 2)

Paul is giving the Corinthians a few strokes in this verse—a warm pat on the back. He expresses his confidence in them and tells how he brags on them to the Macedonians. He goes on to say how their enthusiasm has spread to the church in Achaia. That ability to spread excitement and spur on activity is an important characteristic of a leader.

Alan Loy McGinnis, in *Bringing Out the Best in People,* writes:

> A proven motivator will make it to the top before a proven genius. When Andrew Carnegie hired Charles Schwab to administer his far-flung steel empire, Schwab became the first man in history to earn a million dollars a year while in someone else's employ. Schwab was once asked what equipped him to earn $3000 a day. Was it his knowledge of steel manufacturing? "Nonsense," snorted Schwab. "I have lots of men working for me who know more about steel than I do." Schwab was paid such a handsome amount largely because of his ability to inspire other people. "I consider my ability to arouse enthusiasm among the men the greatest asset I possess," he said, and any leader who can do that can go almost anywhere and name almost any price. [2]

In verse 3, Paul's emphasis shifts back to himself.

> But I have sent the brethren, that our boasting about you may not be made empty in this case, that, as I was saying, you may be prepared.

Notice that Paul himself is involved in the project—he "sent the brethren." It was his job to choose trustworthy, quality people, men who had personal integrity and public trust, to represent him.

Paul also reaffirms the Corinthians' ability—"our boasting about you." One of Paul's great qualities was that he never criticized one church to another. When he found something to be dealt with and corrected, he addressed that person or that church directly. But when he found something praiseworthy, he affirmed it and passed it on.

Affirmation makes a profound impact on people. Remember that teacher who especially believed in you? Or that boss who said, "Great job on that report. I sure appreciate having you around"? Or the times your parents recognized your efforts to be neat, or polite, or obedient? We're all willing to work overtime for people who praise us.

---

2. Alan Loy McGinnis, *Bringing Out the Best in People,* p. 22.

With verse 4, we return to the Corinthians.

> Lest if any Macedonians come with me and find you
> unprepared, we (not to speak of you) should be put to
> shame by this confidence.

In essence Paul is saying, "Look, guys. I've been telling those Macedonians what kind of people you are, how generous and enthusiastic and willing to give. Can you imagine how I'm gonna feel if I have to look 'em in the eye and tell 'em you didn't get around to taking the collection? Let alone how embarrassed you're going to be!" Paul is appealing to the Corinthians' intrinsic motivation to live up to their reputation—as well as their desire to save face!

Verse 5 bounces us back to Paul.

> So I thought it necessary to urge the brethren that
> they would go on ahead to you and arrange beforehand
> your previously promised bountiful gift, that the same
> might be ready as a bountiful gift, and not affected by
> covetousness.

Paul knew the tendency of all of us to part with only the bare minimum and call the job done. And he knew we all struggle with procrastination. This verse is a gentle reminder that blessings come with bountiful giving, and that the Corinthians shouldn't wait until the last minute to collect the money for the gift.

Illustrated

In verse 6, Paul shifts from his specific message to the Corinthians to a general message for everyone.

> Now this I say, he who sows sparingly shall also reap
> sparingly; and he who sows bountifully shall also reap
> bountifully.

Now that's a principle to remember! But it's also one that's been given a lot of false advertising in recent years. God never promises to match you dollar for dollar, or even to reward you in kind. What He promises are the blessings of the heart—the joy of knowing you're obedient, the pleasure of peace, the good feeling of having a part in His work.

The Practical Steps of Involvement

The Corinthians were involved in a project important enough to be written up in Scripture. But we, too, have opportunities for involvement. How can we make the most of them? This takes us right back where we started.

First: *Become an active participant.* Move out of the realm of theory and get into the realm of action. Stop studying about giving— start giving!

Second: *Understand the stated objectives.* God makes His guidelines for giving pretty clear throughout Scripture, beginning with the idea of the tithe in the Old Testament. Take some time to search out the other principles available to you in God's Word, for help in your decisions to give.

Third: *Demonstrate strong enthusiasm.* Don't give grudgingly— give with enthusiasm! It's contagious.

Fourth: *Remember the promised rewards.* God's going to honor you for your active, enthusiastic, knowledgeable involvement with His causes. He'll never just use you up and throw you away!

As you consider applying these guidelines in your own life, take some time to consider how Christ demonstrated them while He was on earth. He was an active participant in the mission of salvation; He never lost sight of His goal; He spread enthusiasm for His cause. And the reward? Every day, people are coming to know Him.

> Who for the joy set before Him endured the cross, despising the shame, and has sat down at the right hand of the throne of God. (Heb. 12:2b)

These principles apply to all of us. How are you fitting them into your life?

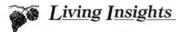 *Living Insights*

Chapters 8 and 9 of 2 Corinthians speak so eloquently to the issue of giving. It would be a shame to hurry through these helpful words. Let's do something to slow down our pace.

- Find a different version of the Bible and read 2 Corinthians 8 and 9. You'll be amazed at the fresh insight this will bring to the subject. Consider a different translation such as the King James Version, New King James Version, Revised Standard Version, New American Standard Bible, or New International Version. Or perhaps a paraphrase like Phillips' New Testament in Modern English or The Living Bible will be helpful.

Are you active in projects that involve giving? Let's take another look at the four steps of involvement we studied in our lesson and see how they apply to our own situations.

• Choose a project you're interested in, and evaluate your involvement according to each statement written below. Check the appropriate box. When you've finished, write out a brief strategy for improving your weaker areas.

I am an active participant.   ☐ Weak   ☐ Average   ☐ Strong

I understand stated   ☐ Weak   ☐ Average   ☐ Strong
objectives.

I demonstrate strong   ☐ Weak   ☐ Average   ☐ Strong
enthusiasm.

I remember promised   ☐ Weak   ☐ Average   ☐ Strong
rewards.

Strategy for Strengthening Involvement

_____

_____

_____

_____

_____

_____

_____

_____

_____

_____

_____

_____

_____

Chapter 4

GIVING BY GRACE

2 Corinthians 9:6–15

A mazing grace! how sweet the sound, / That saved a wretch like me!" These lyrics were born out of the wayward, free-versed life of John Newton.

Newton's godly mother died when he was only seven. He was turned over to relatives and soon forgot the Scriptures she had taught him.

He went on to become an apprentice seaman and later joined the British navy. By then he had earned the reputation of being able to curse for two hours straight without repeating a word. Because he couldn't stand the navy's discipline, he deserted, fleeing to Africa so that, in his own words, "I might sin my fill."

And he did.

Debauched and distant from God, Newton fell into the hands of a Portuguese slave trader. For months the chief woman of the trader's harem treated him like an animal, beating him and forcing him to grovel in the dirt for his food.

By now a gaunt rail of a man, the angry Newton escaped and found his way to the shores of Africa. There he was picked up by a passing ship. Because he was a skilled navigator, he earned the position of first mate. But while the captain was ashore one day, Newton broke out the ship's rum and got the entire crew drunk. When the captain came back, he was so incensed he hit Newton, knocking him overboard.

Newton would have drowned were it not for a sailor who pulled him back on the boat by spearing his thigh with a boat hook. The wound was so immense that it left a scar big enough for Newton to put his fist in. Some weeks later, when the ship neared the coast of Scotland, it sailed into a storm and almost sank. Manning the pumps was the wounded Newton.

Then and there he cried out to God.

God answered that helpless, wretched cry, and later John Newton would emerge from the hold of that ship to become chaplain to England's Parliament and even to preach before the king.

It was this vile blasphemer whom many would later refer to as the second founder of the Church of England. And it was he who wrote: "Amazing grace! how sweet the sound, / That saved a wretch like me! / I once was lost, but now am found, / Was blind, but now I see."[1] And to Newton's ears, there was no sweeter sound in all the world.

A Few Thoughts on Grace

The only way to touch a wretch is through grace. Grace doesn't point a condemning finger or read us the riot act. Grace comes to us in the darkness and accepts us in our sin.

A few thoughts come to mind when thinking of grace. First: *Grace stoops to where we are and lifts us to where we ought to be.* God lifted John Newton from the swamp of a wretched life, just as He did David.

> I waited patiently for the Lord;
> And He inclined to me, and heard my cry.
> He brought me up out of the pit of destruction, out
>   of the miry clay;
> And He set my feet upon a rock making my footsteps
>   firm.
> And He put a new song in my mouth, a song of praise
>   to our God;
> Many will see and fear,
> And will trust in the Lord. (Ps. 40:1–3)

And as surely and soundly as God put David on solid ground, He can do the same for you.

Second: *Grace softens the harsh demands of the Law and offers hope to go on.* Remember the self-righteous religious leaders with stones in their hands, eager to sacrifice a helpless sinner on the unforgiving altar of the Law? And do you remember the response of the Savior?

> "He who is without sin among you, let him be the first
> to throw a stone at her." And again He stooped down,
> and wrote on the ground. And when they heard it,
> they began to go out one by one, beginning with the
> older ones, and He was left alone, and the woman,
> where she had been, in the midst. And straightening

1. Lyrics to "Amazing Grace" and story of John Newton taken from *God's Grace, God's Freedom, God's Heirs*, by Donald Grey Barnhouse (1959, 1961, 1963; reprint, Grand Rapids, Mich.: William B. Eerdmans Publishing Co., 1973), vol. 3, pp. 127–29.

up, Jesus said to her, "Woman, where are they? Did no one condemn you?" And she said, "No one, Lord." And Jesus said, "Neither do I condemn you; go your way. From now on sin no more." (John 8:7b–11)

What gave this woman the motivation to go on her way and sin no more was that Jesus had graciously forgiven her.

Third: *Grace becomes our guide in responding to God and others.* Grace is always greater than our own resources, our own pain, our own need, even our own sin.

"Come now, and let us reason together,"
Says the Lord,
"Though your sins are as scarlet,
They will be as white as snow;
Though they are red like crimson,
They will be like wool." (Isa. 1:18)

This abundance of grace is what overwhelms us with gratitude and changes our relationship with God and others (see Luke 7:36–47).

Specific Applications of Grace

In spite of how amazingly God has shed His favor on us, most of us don't respond as appreciatively and as wholeheartedly as John Newton did. Most of us hold back, especially with regard to our financial stewardship. But in our passage in 2 Corinthians 9:6–15, Paul encourages us to pass on His grace to others.

Bountiful Sowing

In verse 6, the apostle draws upon an agricultural metaphor to illustrate a spiritual truth.

Now this I say, he who sows sparingly shall also reap sparingly; and he who sows bountifully shall also reap bountifully.

Scant sowing makes for scant harvest. Generous sowing, however, makes for an abundant harvest, as Solomon writes in Proverbs 11:24.

It is possible to give away and become richer! It is also possible to hold on too tightly and lose everything. (LB)

Later in Proverbs he writes: "He who is generous will be blessed" (22:9a). This truth is described graphically by Jesus Himself.

"Give, and it will be given to you; good measure, pressed down, shaken together, running over, they will pour

into your lap. For by your standard of measure it will
be measured to you in return." (Luke 6:38)

Cheerful Giving

In verse 7 of 2 Corinthians 9, Paul takes the general principle
of verse 6 and makes it personal.

> Let each one do just as he has purposed in his heart;
> not grudgingly or under compulsion; for God loves a
> cheerful giver.

"Let each one"—that's us. "Just as he has purposed"—or planned.
The Greek term for *purposed* means to "choose beforehand, to decide
ahead of time." This planning should originate not from external
pressures but from within, "in his heart." Gracious giving is the
result of heartfelt resolve. If it isn't from the heart, it is given "grudgingly or under compulsion." But when giving is from a heart full of
cheer, it evokes not only the attention of God but also His love.

Liberal Providing

In verses 8–11, Paul moves the focus off of us and onto God, off
of the immediate giver and onto the ultimate giver.

> God is able to make all grace abound to you, that
> always having all sufficiency in everything, you may
> have an abundance for every good deed; as it is written,
> > "He scattered abroad, he gave to the poor,
> > His righteousness abides forever."
> Now He who supplies seed to the sower and bread for
> food, will supply and multiply your seed for sowing and
> increase the harvest of your righteousness; you will be
> enriched in everything for all liberality, which through
> us is producing thanksgiving to God.

The storehouse of all good things belongs to God (see James
1:17). From that infinite source of blessing, He can replenish all the
seed we ever sow, whether that seed is material or spiritual. And
back in 2 Corinthians 9:10 we are told that God not only will supply
the seed, He will even multiply it.

Joyful Response

In 2 Corinthians 9:12–14, Paul encourages the Corinthian church
to give by helping them see that giving evokes a reciprocal blessing.

> For the ministry of this service is not only fully supply-
> ing the needs of the saints, but is also overflowing

through many thanksgivings to God. Because of the proof given by this ministry they will glorify God for your obedience to your confession of the gospel of Christ, and for the liberality of your contribution to them and to all, while they also, by prayer on your behalf, yearn for you because of the surpassing grace of God in you.

Those who give in grace, seeking no credit for themselves, glorify God. And those who receive in grace, realizing how unworthy they are, also glorify God. The result? The entire process inundates heaven with a high tide of praise, surging at the feet of the Lord.

Can you remember a time when you were really up against the wall financially? A time when your thoughts were turned inward and your pockets outward? A time when you were not only unable to help yourself but also unworthy of being helped by others? And then, from a source you never expected, help came. That's grace. That's why, in John Newton's words, it's amazing.

No matter how deep your sin, grace is deeper. No matter how broad, grace is broader. No matter how high, grace is higher.

And the Law came in that the transgression might increase; but where sin increased, grace abounded all the more. (Rom. 5:20)

That was the life verse of John Bunyan, author of the immortal *Pilgrim's Progress*. In fact, he alludes to that verse in his biography, *Grace Abounding to the Chief of Sinners*.

Amazing grace. Abounding grace. Those who give by grace give the way God does. Always to the undeserving. Always more than is needed.

An Indescribable Gift of Grace

Paul closes chapter 9 with a sudden outpouring of gratitude to God for His grace.

Thanks be to God for His indescribable gift! (v. 15)

Max Lucado, in his tender book *No Wonder They Call Him the Savior*, tells a story that illustrates the indescribable grace of God toward His prodigal children. The story is about a loving mother named Maria and her daughter Christina.

Longing to leave her poor Brazilian neighborhood, Christina wanted to see the world. Discontent with a home having only a pallet on the floor, a washbasin, and a wood-burning stove, she dreamed of a better life in the city. One morning she slipped away, breaking her mother's heart. Knowing what life on the streets would be like for her young, attractive daughter, Maria hurriedly packed to go find her.

On her way to the bus stop she entered a drugstore to get one last thing. Pictures. She sat in the photograph booth, closed the curtain, and spent all she could on pictures of herself. With her purse full of small black-and-white photos, she boarded the next bus to Rio de Janeiro.

Maria knew Christina had no way of earning money. She also knew that her daughter was too stubborn to give up. When pride meets hunger, a human will do things that were before unthinkable. Knowing this, Maria began her search. Bars, hotels, nightclubs, any place with the reputation for street walkers or prostitutes. She went to them all. And at each place she left her picture—taped on a bathroom mirror, tacked to a hotel bulletin board, fastened to a corner phone booth. And on the back of each photo she wrote a note.

It wasn't too long before both the money and the pictures ran out, and Maria had to go home. The weary mother wept as the bus began its long journey back to her small village.

It was a few weeks later that young Christina descended the hotel stairs. Her young face was tired. Her brown eyes no longer danced with youth but spoke of pain and fear. Her laughter was broken. Her dream had become a nightmare. A thousand times over she had longed to trade these countless beds for her secure pallet. Yet the little village was, in too many ways, too far away.

As she reached the bottom of the stairs, her eyes noticed a familiar face. She looked again, and there on the lobby mirror was a small picture of her mother. Christina's eyes burned and her throat tightened as she walked across the room and removed the small photo. Written on the back was this compelling invitation. "Whatever you have done, whatever you have become, it doesn't matter. Please come home."

She did. [2]

2. Max Lucado, *No Wonder They Call Him the Savior* (Portland, Oreg.: Multnomah Press, 1986), pp. 158–59. Used by permission.

The picture God has placed throughout the Scriptures is Jesus hanging on a wooden cross. It's God's way of saying, "Whatever you have done, whatever you have become, it doesn't matter. Please come home."

Can you turn away from such a picture of love, such a picture of giving, such a picture of amazing grace? Can you look at such a picture and not be changed, not compelled to give yourself to Him, not compelled to give yourself to others the way He gave Himself to you?

 ## *Living Insights*

There is no more noble theme in all the Scripture than the grace of God. It is a perfume that permeates every page of the Bible. And what a pleasing fragrance it is!

* What's your favorite biblical illustration of God's grace? Noah's ark? God sparing Isaac? The woman at the well? Turn to your favorite account and reread it. Use the space below to write a summary of how God demonstrated His grace in this particular instance.

God's Grace Illustrated

_____

_____

_____

_____

_____

_____

_____

_____

_____

_____

_____

_____

_____

_____

_____

_____

Living Insights STUDY TWO

How do your giving patterns measure up to those addressed in 2 Corinthians? Let's conduct a personal profile of your financial picture.

- What are you doing to follow God's guidelines for giving?

- What are the biggest obstacles you currently face financially?

- Does the Bible address these obstacles? If so, what is said?

- What have you learned most vividly from the last few lessons concerning your finances?

Chapter 5

A BLOODLESS BATTLE NOBODY NOTICES

2 Corinthians 10:1–6

Physical war is only a tangible enactment of a greater, more real war—the battle of the soul. Regarding that invisible war, Donald Barnhouse writes:

> Not even modern wars are fought with great intensity at every moment. World War II had preliminary months that were called "the phony war." The interval between World War II and the inevitable World War III has been called "the cold war." From the human point of view, it may appear that there are similar phases of relaxation of intensity in the invisible war. But in this realm as in the realm of character, "Man looketh upon the outward appearance." There is no truce in the invisible war. There is no armistice in the invisible war. What may appear to be only a skirmish may in reality be a major engagement.[1]

We are all enmeshed in an invisible war, a war strewn with spiritual casualties. Today we're going to take a closer look at that battle—the battle for the mind. For only when we fully understand the battle can we effectively bind up the wounded, release the hostages, and rally those who have retreated.

The Warfare and the Wounded

South America. The Middle East. South Africa. All are battlegrounds where flesh-and-blood enemies clash daily with each other. We see the gunfire on the nightly news. We read of the casualties in the morning paper. We hear about the escalation of conflicts on the radio. And yet they are only metaphors of a far more literal battle.

> Finally, be strong in the Lord, and in the strength of His might. Put on the full armor of God, that you may be able to stand firm against the schemes of the devil. (Eph. 6:10–11)

1. Donald Grey Barnhouse, *The Invisible War* (Grand Rapids, Mich.: Zondervan Publishing House, 1965), p. 137.

The Greek word for "schemes" is *methodeia,* from which we get our word *method.* It means "cunning arts, deceit, treachery." That's the devil's strategy. Consequently, our struggle is not in the physical realm but in the spiritual.

> For our struggle is not against flesh and blood, but against the rulers, against the powers, against the world forces of this darkness, against the spiritual forces of wickedness in the heavenly places. (v. 12)

This verse describes the hierarchy of the satanic army that is bent on our destruction. Demonic activity is both real and relentless. No "R and R" for Satan's army. These soldiers work around the clock, seven days a week, fifty-two weeks a year, year after year. All the more reason to put on the armor of Ephesians 6:13–17. All the more reason to be alert (1 Pet. 5:8).

Another word—*methodeia*—is even more vivid.

> In order that no advantage be taken of us by Satan; for we are not ignorant of his schemes. (2 Cor. 2:11)

Here, the Greek word for "schemes" is not *methodeia* but *noēma.* It means "mind" and is so translated in 2 Corinthians 3:14, 4:4, and 11:3. Basically Paul is saying, "We're not indifferent to Satan's mind games or unaware of his mental attacks." The bloodless battle nobody notices is the mind battle.

Perhaps no book illustrates the schemes of Satan better than *The Screwtape Letters.* In imaginary correspondence between an older devil, Screwtape, and his ambitious young nephew, Wormwood, C. S. Lewis lifts the veil on the inner workings of Satan's dark hierarchy.

> Doubtless, like all young tempters, you are anxious to be able to report spectacular wickedness. But do remember, the only thing that matters is the extent to which you separate the man from the Enemy. It does not matter how small the sins are, provided that their cumulative effect is to edge the man away from the Light and out into the Nothing. Murder is no better than cards if cards can do the trick. Indeed, the safest road to Hell is the gradual one—the gentle slope, soft underfoot, without sudden turnings, without milestones, without signposts.
>
> Your affectionate uncle
> Screwtape[2]

2. C. S. Lewis, *The Screwtape Letters* (reprint; New York, N.Y.: Macmillan Publishing Co., 1961), p. 56.

The Real Battle Then and Now

Turning our attention to 2 Corinthians 10, we'll take a look at the spiritual battle raging during Paul's time.

The Paul-Corinthian Conflict

Unfortunately, we don't have a specific list of the Corinthians' complaints against Paul, but we do have his answers to those complaints in verses 1–2.

> Now I, Paul, myself urge you by the meekness and gentleness of Christ—I who am meek when face to face with you, but bold toward you when absent! I ask that when I am present I may not be bold with the confidence with which I propose to be courageous against some, who regard us as if we walked according to the flesh.

From these two verses, we can deduce the substance of the Corinthians' criticism. The first verse addresses the accusation of hypocrisy. They criticized Paul for being bold with his letters but lacking courage in person. The second verse combats the criticism of fleshly motives. They accused him of walking in the flesh, of impure motives, and manipulative methods.

In spite of their defamatory remarks, Paul approaches the Corinthians with "the meekness and gentleness of Christ." This tone reflects a calm, controlled response to his accusers. And it is with this same conciliatory tone of humility that he concludes his letter.

> For this reason I am writing these things while absent, in order that when present I may not use severity, in accordance with the authority which the Lord gave me, for building up and not for tearing down. (13:10)

The Flesh-Spirit Warfare

Paul takes the barbs of criticism and turns them into bars of iron to reinforce the foundation of his instruction on spiritual warfare.

> For though we walk in the flesh, we do not war according to the flesh, for the weapons of our warfare are not of the flesh, but divinely powerful for the destruction of fortresses. We are destroying speculations and every lofty thing raised up against the knowledge of God, and we are taking every thought captive to the obedience of Christ. (10:3–5)

In biblical days cities were built with defenses to protect them from enemy invasion. The primary structure, consequently, was the wall that surrounded the city. That's why, when Nehemiah returned to Jerusalem to rebuild the city, he started with the wall. That's why, when Jericho was invaded by the Israelites, the strategy centered around bringing down the walls.

To protect against attack, a few high towers were constructed within the wall. During a siege, military intelligence would give commands from these observation towers to those on the wall itself.

That image is in Paul's mind as he compares the spiritual battle. The *fortress* is our mind. *Speculations* represent the wall built around that fortress. This is our overall mindset, our pattern of reasoning, our mental attitude. Not until the Lord penetrates that thick wall of defense can we attain victory over our thoughts. The *lofty things* of verse 5 constitute mental blocks that we have developed over the years. They are what keep us captive and keep us from thinking as Christ would have us think.

God's strategy in the spiritual battle is to take every thought captive, to scale those lofty observation towers and overcome the military strategists that occupy them. In order for the city to be taken, those scheming, defensive thoughts must be captured and brought into submission, one by one.

The Obedience-Disobedience Issue

Lest the Corinthians think he was dodging the issues they raised, Paul states his readiness and willingness to confront them.

> We are ready to punish all disobedience, whenever
> your obedience is complete. (v. 6)

Church discipline cannot be effective unless the congregation cooperates. Paul is willing to be strong in their midst, but they must first be willing to submit to his leadership. In other words, he's saying, "If I have most of you with me, we can clean up this disciplinary issue and get on with the business of victorious living."

Some Survival-Strategy Suggestions

The strategy for survival against the spiritual battle centers around four words: memorize, personalize, analyze, and visualize.

Memorize

To align our thoughts with God's thoughts, we need to place His thoughts into our minds.

Thy word I have treasured in my heart,
That I may not sin against Thee. (Ps. 119:11)

The verb *treasure* connotes not only an act but an attitude—not only placing God's Word in our heart but also placing a high value on it.

My son, if you will receive my sayings,
And treasure my commandments within you,
Make your ear attentive to wisdom,
Incline your heart to understanding;
For if you cry for discernment,
Lift your voice for understanding;
If you seek her as silver,
And search for her as for hidden treasures;
Then you will discern the fear of the Lord,
And discover the knowledge of God. (Prov. 2:1–5)

Are you doing that? Are you hiding God's Word in your heart? Do you value His words as you would a treasure, seeking them with more diligence than you would silver or gold?

Personalize

To replace old, negative, discouraging thoughts with those that are positive, encouraging, and uplifting, insert the personal pronouns I, me, my, or mine into the verses you memorize. For example, take a look at Philippians 4:6–7.

Be anxious for nothing, but in everything by prayer
and supplication with thanksgiving let your requests
be made known to God. And the peace of God, which
surpasses all comprehension, shall guard your hearts
and your minds in Christ Jesus.

Begin applying the passage to your life by first coming up with your own personal paraphrase: I will be anxious for nothing. In every area of my life I will prayerfully let my requests be made known to God. And in the process, God will march sentry duty around the walls of my mind and protect me from anxieties that in the past have captured my thoughts.

Analyze

The Scripture mirrors the complex workings of your inner life (James 1:23–25). Stand before that mirror and ask yourself a few hard questions about what could be holding you back from living victoriously: Is there something or someone I'm afraid of? Why am I defensive? Why am I closed? Do I really want God's will in my present circumstance? How do I respond to peer pressure? Why do I respond that way? Why am I so vulnerable and weak in this area of my life? Is there a blind spot I'm oblivious to?

Visualize

The mind is an incredibly powerful tool whose thoughts, when properly focused, can lift us to new heights. Consider the words of the visionary writer Thoreau:

> If one advances confidently in the direction of his dreams, and endeavors to live the life which he has imagined, he will meet with a success unexpected in common hours.[3]

That quote captures the essence of the Christian life, which isn't a contrived public display. This life is a deep, spontaneous, abiding, spiritual, invisible thing, where through the invasion of the Scripture and the power of the Holy Spirit our Lord overruns our speculations, scales the lofty towers in our minds, and brings every thought captive into obedience to Christ. Then, and only then, will we fully experience the truth. And that truth will make us free (John 8:31–32).

 Living Insights STUDY ONE

The battle for the mind is the bloodless battle nobody notices, a battle carefully explained for us in 2 Corinthians 10:1–6. Let's take a closer look.

- Reread the passage, and jot down nine or ten words you consider key to the text. Then determine the meaning of each word from the context or a Bible dictionary. Finally, write a brief statement on why the word is significant to the passage.

2 Corinthians 10:1–6

Key Word: _____

Meaning: _____

Significance: _____

---

3. Henry David Thoreau, as quoted in *Bartlett's Familiar Quotations,* 14th ed., rev. and enl., ed. Emily Morison Beck (Boston, Mass.: Little, Brown and Co., 1968), p. 683.

Key Word: _____

Meaning: _____

Significance: _____

Key Word: _____

Meaning: _____

Significance: _____

Key Word: _____

Meaning: _____

Significance: _____

Key Word: _____

Meaning: _____

Significance: _____

Key Word: _____

Meaning: _____

Significance: _____

Key Word: _____

Meaning: _____

Significance: _____

Key Word: _____

Meaning: _____

Significance: _____

Key Word: _____

Meaning: _____

Significance: _____

Key Word: _____

Meaning: _____

Significance: _____

One of the purposes of the Living Insights is to bring about a practical, concrete form of application for each lesson. Since today's lesson concerns the battle for our minds, some mental application is certainly in order.

- Take the following passage and run it through the four steps we studied in our lesson.

    Memorize: How blessed is the man who does not walk in the counsel of the wicked,
    Nor stand in the path of sinners,
    Nor sit in the seat of scoffers!
    But his delight is in the law of the Lord,
    And in His law he meditates day and night.
    And he will be like a tree firmly planted by streams of water,
    Which yields its fruit in its season,
    And its leaf does not wither;
    And in whatever he does, he prospers.
    (Ps. 1:1–3)

Personalize: _____

_____

_____

_____

Analyze: _____

_____

_____

_____

Visualize: _____

_____

_____

_____

Chapter 6

Stabilized
Though Criticized
2 Corinthians 10:7–18

S uccess has a spirit-stealing sister—her name is *criticism*. Have
you noticed her hanging around? Just when you've finished a
presentation to the board or an inspiring lecture to your students or
an insightful comment at the PTA, those stinging comments start.
"But don't you think . . . ?" "Have you considered . . . ?" "Well, *I*
would never . . . !"

Sometimes you just want to throw in the towel.

Back in 1899, Teddy Roosevelt wrote some words of encouragement for the criticized that are good to keep in mind.

> It is not the critic who counts; not the man who
> points out how the strong man stumbles, or where the
> doer of deeds could have done them better. The credit
> belongs to the man who is actually in the arena, whose
> face is marred by dust and sweat and blood; who strives
> valiantly; who errs, and comes short again and again,
> because there is no effort without error and shortcom-
> ing; but who does actually strive to do the deeds; who
> knows the great enthusiasms, the great devotions; who
> spends himself in a worthy cause; who at the best
> knows in the end the triumph of high achievement,
> and who at the worst, if he fails, at least fails while
> daring greatly.[1]

One of the crucial questions in life, whether you're entering
marriage or the ministry or a profession, is, How well do you handle
criticism? Because it's going to come. Sometimes it'll be construc-
tive, sometimes destructive. But it'll be there, and you need to be
ready for it.

---

1. Theodore Roosevelt, from the speech "Citizen in a Republic," given at the Sor-
bonne, Paris, France, April 23, 1910, as quoted in *The Man in the Arena*, ed. John
Allen Gable (Oyster Bay, N.Y.: Theodore Roosevelt Association, 1987), p. 54.

Facts about Criticism We Must Remember

Sometimes criticism comes gently from a sincere heart. But the remarks that hurt us most come from carping, caustic critics whose words fly like arrows from bows of opinion or ignorance.

We've all been stung by criticism's barbed words. Let's look now at three principles that can help take the edge off the pain.

No one is immune to criticism.

Criticism is an unavoidable part of living among human beings. So since we can't escape it, why not expect it, get ready for it? Criticism doesn't have to come as a surprise attack. And if you prepare yourself for its onslaught, you'll be less likely to feel like quitting or fighting back.

When you see criticism coming, yield to the experience. Don't flinch in fear like a child fighting off a shot at the doctor's office. And don't flex your muscles to protect yourself from its sting. Relax and yield to its needle.

Criticism can be taken too lightly or too seriously.

Knowing how to take criticism is like trying to balance a teeter-totter by yourself—just a little too far to one end or the other and you're likely to end up with a skinned knee.

If we take criticism lightly, we may miss out on some valuable instruction. Where would we be without our parents' correction? Or without that close friend to point out our blind spots?

On the other hand, if we take criticism too seriously, we may lose heart. We might eventually decide never to dream again, or to quit before the task is done. Or we may become intimidated, tenuous, insecure, emotionally crippled.

A balanced approach is to take criticism to heart, but to take it with a grain of salt. Like one man has said,

> What people say about us is never quite true; but it is never quite false, either; they always miss the bull's-eye, but they rarely fail to hit the target.[2]

Some criticism needs to be answered; much of it does not.

Some people are so convinced they're right that they never read critical mail, and they surround themselves with people who never

---

2. Sydney Harris, as quoted in *Quote Unquote*, comp. Lloyd Cory (Wheaton, Ill.: SP Publications, Victor Books, 1977), p. 79.

question their decisions. They've built a protective wall around themselves so thick no critical words can penetrate, not even wise ones. Not only are these people unresponsive to criticism; they don't even hear it.

There are other people, though, who pore over every suggestion, apologize profusely over every complaint, scramble to please, and fret about each minute disagreement.

Where can you place the fulcrum to achieve a perfect balance? You can start by analyzing the problem.

If the criticism is based on a misunderstanding, clear it up. If the critic is willing to look through your glasses and is open to discussion, hold a meeting of the minds. And if good might come from an exchange of thoughts, put your heads together.

But if responding would only lead to more argument . . . if the critic is a chronic grouch . . . if it is virtually impossible to address the one who originated the criticism—let it rest!

Jesus, on occasion, answered criticism directly and quickly. But more often than not, He met His critics with silence . . . even when their critical hands nailed Him to the cross.

Areas of Criticism Leveled against Paul

As we study the last twelve verses of 2 Corinthians 10, we'll see Paul dive headfirst into the subject of criticism. A close look at this chapter shows us that at least three critical remarks had been fired at Paul.

"Paul, you're a hypocrite!"

The apostle opens this section of his letter with what appears to be a sarcastic remark.

> Now I, Paul, myself urge you by the meekness and gentleness of Christ—I who am meek when face to face with you, but bold toward you when absent! (v. 1)

Apparently, some people had been criticizing Paul's style. They thought he was hiding behind his correspondence, trying to present himself as a leader with backbone when in person he was spineless as a jellyfish—in other words, a hypocrite.[3]

3. Our word *hypocrite* comes from the Greek word *hypocritos*, "one who speaks from behind a mask." It was used to refer to the actors in ancient Greek plays who played both comic and tragic roles. The actors would don masks—smiling masks for their lines of comedy, and sad masks for their lines of tragedy.

"Paul, you're overemphasizing your authority!"

Some people were also critical of his role of authority over them.

> For even if I should boast somewhat further about our authority, which the Lord gave for building you up and not for destroying you, I shall not be put to shame. (v. 8)

These people seemed to resent Paul's leadership, even though it had been given to him by God. Ever been in a similar position? Maybe you've been promoted when others have been passed by. Or maybe you've been asked to teach a Sunday School class or take over leadership of your Bible study group. You've been chosen as the leader, but not everyone is willing to follow.

"Paul, you're unimpressive in appearance and you're not that great to listen to!"

This was the most superficial criticism of all. The Living Bible says it best:

> "He sounds big, but it's all noise. When he gets here you will see that there is nothing great about him, and you have never heard a worse preacher!" (v. 10)

The critics showed their shallowness with this criticism, but its pain cut deep. Of all their complaints, only this one had a ring of truth, as echoed by an Asian presbyter during the second century.

> [Paul was] a man small of stature, with a bald head and crooked legs, in a good state of body, with eyebrows meeting and nose somewhat hooked.[4]

From all accounts, it's doubtful that Paul was a handsome man. But never be misled about the vessels in which God places His riches—after all,

> God sees not as man sees, for man looks at the outward appearance, but the Lord looks at the heart. (1 Sam. 16:7b)

Response to Criticism: Four Thoughtful Answers

As we work our way through the rest of 2 Corinthians 10, we find four reasonable, calm answers from this unintimidated servant of Christ.

---

4. As quoted in *The Ministry and Message of Paul,* by Richard Longenecker (Grand Rapids, Mich.: Zondervan Publishing House, 1971), p. 23.

First: *He corrects their perspective.* Paul's response to attack is gentle but firm. In verse 7a, he gets right to the heart of the problem.

You are looking at things as they are outwardly.

One of the reasons people criticize is that they don't look deep enough. They haven't peered below the surface or stood in the other's shoes. This was true in the Corinthians' case.

Parenthetically, there's also an application to the one *being* criticized: Before you take offense at a reproachful remark, take a look at yourself from the critic's perspective. You may still disagree, but understanding the other viewpoint may take some of the sting out of the statement.

Second: *He clarifies his motive.* Paul makes sure his critics understand what's in his heart.

> For even if I should boast somewhat further about our
> authority, which the Lord gave for building you up and
> not for destroying you, I shall not be put to shame,
> for I do not wish to seem as if I would terrify you by
> my letters. (vv. 8–9)

Don't assume people know why you do what you do. Help them understand your reasoning. Be vulnerable enough for them to see your perspective or feel your pain. And try to understand why they feel the way they do, even if you believe their feelings are groundless.

Third: *He confesses his authenticity.* Paul assures the Corinthians that he is just the way he presents himself. What you see is what you get.

> Let such a person consider this, that what we are in
> word by letters when absent, such persons we are also
> in deed when present. For we are not bold to class or
> compare ourselves with some of those who commend
> themselves; but when they measure themselves by
> themselves, and compare themselves with themselves,
> they are without understanding. (vv. 11–12)

The Corinthians' accusations were unfounded; Paul was just being himself, through and through. But not everyone can make that claim. If you are not authentic—if you are presenting yourself to be something you really are not—you may be inviting justifiable criticism.

Fourth: *He communicates the facts.* Paul reiterates four crucial facts about his ministry.

> But we will not boast beyond our measure, but within
> the measure of the sphere which God apportioned to

us as a measure, to reach even as far as you. For we are not overextending ourselves, as if we did not reach to you, for we were the first to come even as far as you in the gospel of Christ; not boasting beyond our measure, that is, in other men's labors, but with the hope that as your faith grows, we shall be, within our sphere, enlarged even more by you, so as to preach the gospel even to the regions beyond you. (vv. 13–16a)

There's nothing quite like solid facts to comfort us during times of criticism. Possibly Paul included this paragraph as much for his own reassurance as for theirs.

First, he reminds them that his ministry is given to him by God (v. 13) and that his reason for coming to Corinth was to bring them the good news (v. 14). He also reminds them that he never lorded his leadership over them—on the contrary, he looked forward to learning from them (v. 15).

Paul also recalls that Corinth isn't his only place of ministry; his involvement extends "even to regions beyond" (v. 16a). If he had been holding on to that ministry so tightly that losing it would affect his ego, the Corinthians would have good reason to want to wriggle free. But Paul's ministry was spread like fingers all over the region, and his fist wasn't clenched over any one area.

Recovering from Criticism: Three Helpful Reminders

It's one thing to read about Paul's response to criticism; it's quite another thing to keep your own cool when critics turn up the heat! Let's take a look at three suggestions to help give us staying power when the critical steam in the kitchen gets too hot.

Openly claim your own responsibility.

Three of the hardest words in the English language are *you are right*. The flip side of those words—*I am wrong*—is equally difficult. When a critic's words ring true—even a little bit—admit it, own up to it. That's how we grow.

Humbly stand where you know you're right.

When you've examined the reproach and you're still sure you're right, stand firm. Don't let others budge you from what you're sure God has called you to do or be. But resist with humility. As Paul did, "boast in the Lord"—not in yourself.

Calmly allow the Lord to defend you.

This is especially important when you have reached an impasse, when you can say or do nothing more. God will take care of you. He knows the truth, and He won't forsake you.

 *Living Insights*

We've been studying criticism from the perspective of the criticized. Let's take another approach and examine what the Bible says about how we use our tongues.

- Skim the first nine chapters of Proverbs. Using the chart below, note any verses you find that refer to the way we speak. Summarize what you discover from each verse.

Proverbs 1–9: The Power of Our Tongues	
References	Summaries

We've seen how Paul dealt with criticism. Now let's think about how *we* handle it.

- Write a brief personal history of how you typically deal with criticism. Do you feel your approach is biblical? In what ways has it been effective? In what ways has it been ineffective? Include some ideas you have gained from our lesson today.

How I Handle Criticism

_____

_____

_____

_____

_____

_____

_____

_____

_____

_____

_____

_____

_____

_____

_____

_____

_____

_____

_____

Chapter 7

NOT ALL "MINISTRIES" ARE MINISTRIES

2 Corinthians 11:1–15

Donna was dissatisfied with her job and was suffering through a broken engagement when some friends invited her to a Sunday service at a nearby church commune. She was immediately impressed with the friendly, sincere people she met there and began to attend the services regularly.

She recalls those early days: "Each week you would be welcomed by people who remembered your name, and they would be anxious to tell you of the exciting and wonderful things the group had done that past week. You began to think you were really missing something because you hadn't been a part of the activity."

Within a few months, Donna quit her job and moved into the commune. The next two years were the happiest of her life—she had no responsibilities, no worries. Her life was planned for her by the leaders, and all she had to do was obey, like a child. "They insisted that the answer to life lay in renouncing self and all earthly ties to family, friends, and possessions, and by giving oneself entirely to serving God through the special mission of the commune."

Eventually, though, she began to see the group's dark side. Members were allowed little outside contact—no TV, magazines, newspapers. "You had to turn your mind off," she says. The mysterious female pastor was rarely seen, but members were expected to shower her with expensive gifts, proving their love and devotion.

Donna was repeatedly summoned to bizarre secret meetings in the middle of the night where she and others were publicly humiliated and interrogated, under the guise of destroying their sinful pride. She learned that group members achieved status by informing on the others, so "everybody watched everyone else and cut the other guy's throat in order to save his own neck." For the first time, she also became aware of the complex security system and the ever-present guards she once thought were there for her protection.

It took her three years to escape.[1]

1. Story from *The Lure of the Cults and New Religions*, 2d ed., by Ronald Enroth (Downers Grove, Ill.: InterVarsity Press, 1987), pp. 65–74.

How did Donna, a Christian college graduate, get sucked into this insidious cult? Jack Sparks, in his fascinating book *The Mindbenders,* explains that cults use three simultaneous methods to lure their members.

> *Step one* is "deprogramming." Your past is all wrong. No matter how sincere your parents or your church may have been, they were wrong. . . . What you always thought was right is wrong, wrong, wrong, wrong! Reject it. . . .
>
> *Step two* demands your will be captured by the cult. The human will does not function apart from the mind. Thus, if the normal function of the mind can be altered, control of the will can be gained. Habitual patterns of behavior and response will be broken and a new program put in its place. . . .
>
> *Step three* is the concentrated reprogramming phase. Intensive teaching or indoctrination is the prime means. Day after day, like the dripping of rain, the old concepts are methodically dug up and the new ones planted in their place. A whole new structure is raised. In all of this the convert is hardly aware anything is taking place.[2]

False religions have been around as long as there has been true religion. Early in the first century, Jesus had to contend with the scribes and Pharisees, the original legalists. They had bound the Jews with judgment and condemnation, threatening to excommunicate from the synagogue anyone who violated one of their more than six hundred rules and regulations. These rules were not part of the Mosaic Law but merely traditions added to the Law down through the generations.

In this lesson, we'll look first at Jesus' response to the false teachers of His day and then at Paul's warnings to the Corinthians concerning the deception infiltrating their ranks. Because of the multiplicity of cults surrounding us today, these warnings are equally relevant to us.

Red Flags in Questionable Ministries

In Matthew 15:1–14, we see four red flags that signal a questionable ministry.

2. Jack Sparks, *The Mindbenders* (Nashville, Tenn.: Thomas Nelson Publishers, 1977), pp. 16–17.

First: *Questionable ministries substitute human tradition for divine revelation.* The Pharisees have come to Jesus with one of their loaded questions.

> "Why do Your disciples transgress the tradition of the elders? For they do not wash their hands when they eat bread." (v. 2)

How does Jesus answer them? With a pointed question of His own.

> "And why do you yourselves transgress the commandment of God for the sake of your tradition? For God said, 'Honor your father and mother,' and 'He who speaks evil of father or mother, let him be put to death.' But you say, 'Whoever shall say to his father or mother, "Anything of mine you might have been helped by has been given to God," he is not to honor his father or his mother.' And thus you invalidated the word of God for the sake of your tradition." (vv. 3–6)

Invalidate comes from the Greek prefix *a,* meaning "non," and the root *kuros* or *kurios,* meaning "authority" or "Lord." Jesus is saying that the Pharisees had negated the authority of God's Word, substituting their traditions instead.

Second: *Questionable ministries have externals that seem right, but internally they're far from God.* Jesus continues with a sharp rebuke.

> "You hypocrites, rightly did Isaiah prophesy of you, saying,
> ' This people honors Me with their lips,
> But their heart is far away from Me.
> But in vain do they worship Me,
> Teaching as doctrines the precepts of
> men.'" (vv. 7–9)

Cult members may sound right or look right, but don't be fooled. Look deep within, into their hearts and their motives.

Third: *Questionable ministries offer teachings that defile and destroy.*[3] This is revealed in verses 10–11.

> And after He called the multitude to Him, He said to them, "Hear, and understand. Not what enters into the mouth defiles the man, but what proceeds out of the mouth, this defiles the man."

---

3. Conversely, orthodox teaching brings glory to God. In the Greek, *orthos* means "straight, right" and *doxa* means "glory."

What comes from the mouth originates in the heart (see vv. 19–20). The ugly truth of the cults is that their teaching ultimately brings destruction in the form of spiritual ruin, moral compromise, and emotional instability.

Fourth: *Questionable ministries are led by the blind.* "Let them alone," Jesus says. "They are blind guides of the blind. And if a blind man guides a blind man, both will fall into a pit" (v. 14). In other words, these spiritually blind leaders are leading their equally blind followers to hell. Jesus says to stay away from them—don't get sucked into their manipulation.

When you evaluate any religious organization, watch out for six blind spots. Their presence will tell you whether the "ministry" is really a ministry.

1. *Authoritarianism*—lack of a servant's heart, lack of grace
2. *Exclusiveness*—suspicion and paranoia, theirs is the only way
3. *Greed*—manipulation to get money
4. *Sensuality*—moral impurity, sexual looseness
5. *Unaccountability*—secrecy, irresponsibility
6. *Rationalization*—defensiveness when confronted, twisting the Scriptures to fit lifestyle or opinions

The True and the False: Our Need for Discernment

Unfortunately, false teaching continued through the first century, invading the Corinthian church as well. Those teachers accused Paul of heresy, creating a heresy of their own. So in the eleventh chapter of his second letter to these gullible Greeks, Paul warns of the trap awaiting them.

Concern of a Caring Shepherd

Paul explains his distaste for what he has to do in 2 Corinthians 11:1: "Bear with me in a little foolishness." By foolishness, he means having to talk about himself, to boast about his role, to present his credentials, to stress his apostolic authority. Why does he do it then?

> For I am jealous for you with a godly jealousy; for I betrothed you to one husband, that to Christ I might present you as a pure virgin. But I am afraid, lest as the serpent deceived Eve by his craftiness, your minds should be led astray from the simplicity and purity of devotion to Christ. (vv. 2–3)

He's jealous for their spiritual purity, as a father would be jealous for his daughter's sexual purity before he presents her to her groom. Paul wants to offer to Christ a church with an unadulterated loyalty and love for Him.

Differences between the Authentic and the Artificial

In verses 4–12, Paul contrasts the true and the false, showing the Corinthians three ways to know the difference.

> For if one comes and preaches *another* Jesus whom we have not preached, or you receive a *different* spirit which you have not received, or a *different* gospel which you have not accepted, you bear this beautifully. (vv. 4–5, emphasis added)

Difference number one: *False teachers proclaim another Jesus and a different gospel. Another* here means "another of a similar kind." A false teacher may talk about Jesus, he may sound biblical, but he's fooling you. *Different,* on the other hand, means "another of an opposite kind." Their spirit is opposite to the Spirit of Christ, creating divisiveness. And their gospel opposes the gospel of salvation, usually adding works. But "you bear this beautifully," Paul says with a touch of sarcasm, meaning they were tolerant of this heresy.

Difference number two: *False teachers have a lot of charisma.* The Corinthians were persuaded to embrace heretical teaching because it was wrapped in appealing charm. Now Paul begins his defense.

> For I consider myself not in the least inferior to the most eminent apostles. But even if I am unskilled in speech, yet I am not so in knowledge; in fact, in every way we have made this evident to you in all things. (vv. 5–6)

Basically his argument is this: "I'm just as authentic as the original twelve apostles. Place me next to Peter, Andrew, James, or John, and I can measure up with the best of them. Others may be more eloquent, but what I lack in eloquence, I more than compensate for in knowledge, for God has taught me what I'm teaching you."

Don't be seduced by persuasive delivery—check the content.

Difference number three: *False teachers are greedy.* Some of these teachers were telling the Corinthians that Paul's words weren't worth hearing because he didn't charge an admission fee. Paul addresses that accusation in verses 7–9.

> Did I commit a sin in humbling myself that you might be exalted, because I preached the gospel of God to you without charge? I robbed other churches, taking wages from them to serve you; and when I was present with you and was in need, I was not a burden to anyone; for when the brethren came from Macedonia, they fully supplied my need, and in everything I kept myself from being a burden to you, and will continue to do so.

Paul had received offerings from other churches so that he could remain financially free in wealthy Corinth; he never wanted it said that he came to them for the money they could have amply provided. [4]

Paul concludes his personal defense in verses 10–12.

> As the truth of Christ is in me, this boasting of mine will not be stopped in the regions of Achaia. Why? Because I do not love you? God knows I do! But what I am doing, I will continue to do, that I may cut off opportunity from those who desire an opportunity to be regarded just as we are in the matter about which they are boasting.

Because of his love for the Corinthians, Paul will continue to point out these wolves in sheep's clothing (see Matt. 7:15, Acts 20:29).

Reason Behind the Lure of False "Ministries"

Was Paul surprised by the popularity of these false teachers? No, for he knew their source.

> For such men are false apostles, deceitful workers, disguising themselves as apostles of Christ. And no wonder, for even Satan disguises himself as an angel of light. Therefore it is not surprising if his servants also disguise themselves as servants of righteousness. (2 Cor. 11:13–15a)

Satan—the archenemy of Christ Himself—was behind it all. How does he do it? He *disguises* himself. The word means "to change in fashion or appearance" and has the idea of a masquerade. Satan and his followers may appear right and good at first. But their "end shall be according to their deeds" (v. 15b). They'll fall victim to their own lies and will perish without Christ.

---

4. Peter also warns against greed in 1 Peter 5:1–4: "Shepherd the flock of God . . . not for sordid gain, but with eagerness" (v. 2).

To Keep from Falling for the Phony . . .

Here are two suggestions to help you discern authentic ministries from the artificial.

First: *Probe into the doctrinal statement of the organization.* Does it proclaim the deity of Jesus Christ as the eternal second member of the Trinity? And does it offer salvation as a free gift of God, purchased at the cross by Christ and available without works, based on His death and bodily resurrection? If anything's missing, leave it alone—it's heresy.

Second: *Examine the private lives of leadership.* Are the leaders accountable? Do they have servants' hearts? Are they free from sexual and moral impurity? Free of greed and financial impropriety? Willing to answer hard questions openly and honestly?

Remember, you have a message of hope based on Jesus Christ and the Bible. When you come into contact with a cult member, share that message. Stay on the offensive—know your Bible, stick to the issues of Christ and salvation, pray that this person will respond. But don't entertain their doctrine, for what may look like a pot of gold at the end of the rainbow is really a coiled viper waiting to poison you.

Living Insights   STUDY ONE

This lesson is extremely relevant to us today—it's essential for us to be able to discern between authentic and artificial ministries. Let's spend more time with this passage.

* The heart of this text is worth memorizing. On an index card write out verses 3–4 of 2 Corinthians 11. Then read them aloud over and over. Before you know it, you'll be relying less on your card and more on your memory.

Living Insights   STUDY TWO

What kinds of ministries appeal to you? Do you financially support one or more? What are your criteria for supporting a ministry? Why not take a few minutes to seriously consider the two questions that follow for each of the ministries you are involved with.

* What do I know about the doctrinal beliefs of this organization?
* What do I know about its leadership?

Chapter 8

THE FLIP SIDE OF "FANTASTIC"

2 Corinthians 11:16–33

R eal life is not always fantastic. Even the best of Christians are not immune to abrasive rubs with reality. For disaster, disease, and death touch the Christian as often as anyone else.

Most of us try to present a cheery demeanor when life is crumbling all around us. Ask us how we're doing, and we say "Fine!" . . . "Great!" . . . "Fantastic!"

Maybe we're trying the best we can to keep faith; maybe the pain of our circumstances causes us to suppress our true feelings; maybe pride makes us hide behind an I'm-on-top-of-things mask; or maybe, just maybe, we're trying to spare others the pain and disillusionment we're feeling inside.

For whatever reason, when we put on a false face, we mask reality and create a false impression of our lives. How much better it would be, when people ask how we are doing, to tell them the truth. To tell them "I'm learning" or "I'm growing," instead of "Great" or "Fantastic." That type of answer doesn't mean that Christ isn't Lord or that God doesn't provide or that we don't have a magnificent future awaiting us. It simply means that life is so much more than a happy-go-lucky existence.

Real life is the flip side to the stuck recording of "fantastic." Sometimes real life carries a downbeat tune. Sometimes it's scratchy. Sometimes it sounds flat or even repugnant. But at least it proclaims the truth. That's integrity. That's real life. And that's where we should be living.

A Good Response to "How Ya Doin'?"

Romans 5 gives us a good outline to use when someone asks us how we're doing.

> Therefore having been justified by faith, we have peace
> with God through our Lord Jesus Christ. (v. 1)

Our first response to that question should be: *I have peace with God*. Being justified by faith brings peace with the Judge of the universe. Our second answer is found in verse 2.

> Through whom also we have obtained our introduction
> by faith into this grace in which we stand; and we
> exult in hope of the glory of God.

Not only do I have peace with God, *I have the hope of the glory of God.* Standing in grace brings a hope that causes us to exult in God's glory. As a result, we can also exult even in the midst of excruciating circumstances.

> And not only this, but we also exult in our tribula-
> tions, knowing that tribulation brings about persever-
> ance; and perseverance, proven character; and proven
> character, hope; and hope does not disappoint, be-
> cause the love of God has been poured out within our
> hearts through the Holy Spirit who was given to us.
> (vv. 3–5)

The third answer to the question, "How ya doin'?" is: *I'm inundated with the love of God.*

The same man who wrote those great doctrinal thoughts to the Romans also unveiled his personal life to the Corinthians. In this second letter to the church at Corinth, we get an inside glimpse of the flip side of his life. As we will see, it was often less than fantastic.

An Honest Reaction to "What About Them?"

When Paul left the Corinthian church, it created a vacuum of sound leadership quickly filled by false teachers. In they came, looking better than Paul looked, preaching better than Paul preached, and with more impressive credentials than Paul had. As a result, Paul resorts to a little boasting of his own in 2 Corinthians 11:1–6, which he refers to as "a little foolishness."

The dazzling impression these teachers made on the church prompted Paul to assert his credentials in 11:16–33. In verses 16–19 he humbly apologizes for the bold assertion, but he then goes on to chalk a dark character sketch of the false teachers.

> For you bear with anyone if he enslaves you, if he
> devours you, if he takes advantage of you, if he exalts
> himself, if he hits you in the face. (v. 20)

The problem the Corinthians had was one of discernment. As you reflect on this passage, examine your own discernment. Can you separate doctrinal wheat from chaff? Can you spot a wolf in clerical clothing?

Compared to the false teachers, Paul states that he was weak (v. 21); he didn't have the charisma they did. His credentials, however, stacked up higher than theirs.

> Are they Hebrews? So am I. Are they Israelites? So am I. Are they descendants of Abraham? So am I. Are they servants of Christ? (I speak as if insane) I more so. (vv. 22–23a)

The false teachers had their own set of impressive credentials. But they didn't have the credentials that counted in the eyes of God—a heart of sincere devotion and sacrificial service. Sadly, though, the Corinthians didn't have the discernment to see that. They had become enslaved to these masters of rhetoric and oration. They had become impressed with the external sparkle of their polish and pedigrees.

Invariably, becoming enamored with externals leads us away from the path of simple devotion to Christ. We have a propensity for focusing on outward appearance rather than inner commitment (see 1 Sam. 16:7). We are attracted to the glint of accomplishment, the shine of degrees, the sparkle of titles. But in the final assay, these are only fool's gold. The real gold is the hidden treasure of a heart totally devoted to Christ—a heart like the apostle Paul's.

A Realistic Portrayal of "What's It Like?"

Instead of boasting about his victories, Paul delineates his defeats.

> In far more labors, in far more imprisonments, beaten times without number, often in danger of death. Five times I received from the Jews thirty-nine lashes. Three times I was beaten with rods, once I was stoned, three times I was shipwrecked, a night and a day I have spent in the deep. I have been on frequent journeys, in dangers from rivers, dangers from robbers, dangers from my countrymen, dangers from the Gentiles, dangers in the city, dangers in the wilderness, dangers on the sea, dangers among false brethren; I have been in labor and hardship, through many sleepless nights, in hunger and thirst, often without food, in cold and exposure. (2 Cor. 11:23b–27)

Scar by scar, Paul shows the Corinthians his battle wounds. Each tells a story of genuine devotion to Christ, a sharp contrast to the false teachers, who have come through the Christian life relatively unscathed. And, tangentially, he establishes the fact that the Christian life is less than fantastic. It is filled with pain and heartache and uncertainty. It is a winding, uphill path with sharp stones under-foot. It is, in essence, the way of the cross. But it is a path that Jesus walked before us (Heb. 12:2–3, 1 Pet. 2:21). And it is a path trodden by the feet of the saints of whom the world was not worthy (Heb. 11:35–38).

If all these crushing circumstances weren't enough, Paul ached with anxiety—he was a worrier, just like many of us.

> Apart from such external things, there is the daily pressure upon me of concern for all the churches. (2 Cor. 11:28)

Cumulatively, these pressures had molded Paul into the man he was. They made him weak and defenseless, but also empathetic, as verse 29 reveals.

> Who is weak without my being weak? Who is led into sin without my intense concern?

When you've suffered like Paul, your faith is moved out of the theoretical realm and into the practical. It becomes real. When you've been weakened, you understand a person in weakness. You don't look over your critical glasses and ask, "When are you gonna snap out of it?" When you've been there yourself, you're concerned, not condemning.

The final verses in chapter 11 hardly frame a studio portrait of the apostle.

> If I have to boast, I will boast of what pertains to my weakness. The God and Father of the Lord Jesus, He who is blessed forever, knows that I am not lying. In Damascus the ethnarch under Aretas the king was guarding the city of the Damascenes in order to seize me, and I was let down in a basket through a window in the wall, and so escaped his hands. (vv. 30–33)

Nothing fantastic about being dumped in a basket like a sack of rice and let down through a window to flee for your life. No VIP treatment for this servant of Christ. No limo. No Secret Service men.

We hear no clash of the cymbals, no roll of the timpani, no blast of the trumpet. Neither do we see the hero in the limelight of center stage. He's offstage, far from the applause and accolades awarded to the false teachers.

Three things stand out about Paul's description of his credentials, his circumstances, and his character. First, Paul doesn't deny the pain and pressures of life. Never once does he suggest that following Christ is always a fantastic, problem-free life. Second, the apostle doesn't market his misery. It had to be forced out of him. You even get the impression that he found it awkward to talk about himself in these terms. Third, he doesn't explain why. Verse 33 ends abruptly. Paul makes no attempt to analyze or moralize. He doesn't give a three-part outline on why we suffer. All we see at the end of the chapter is a man who is weak and helpless, dropped in a basket from a window, and fleeing for his life.

Eugene Peterson, a pastor who understands suffering, writes poignantly about the role of the pastor in ministering to the hurting.

> When a pastor encounters a person in trouble, the first order of pastoral ministry is to enter into the pain and to share the suffering. Later on the task develops into clearing away the emotional rubble and exposing the historical foundations: all suffering is triggered by something. There is a datable event behind an act of suffering—a remembered word of scorn which wounded, a describable injustice causing injury, a death with a date on it pinpointing the hour of loss, a divorce decree giving legal definition to a rejection. Suffering explodes in a life, and pain is scattered like shrapnel. At the moment the loss seems total, but gradually it is possible to recognize and touch many, many things, persons, areas that remain sound and stable—to discover weakness, to admit guilt, to accept responsibility, to be grateful for survival. But if we fail to maintain a foothold in local history, suffering like a helium-filled balloon lifts us off the ground, and we drift, directionless, through the air at the mercy of emotional air currents and the barometric pressures of hormonal secretions. Sorrow that does not have historical ballast becomes anxiety and turns finally into mental illness or emotional bitterness. History is necessary, not to explain, but to anchor. . . .
>
> . . . Pastoral work joins the sufferer, shares the experience of God's anger, enters into the pain, the hurt, the sense of absurdity, the descent into the depths. It is not the task of the pastor to alleviate suffering, to minimize it, or to mitigate it, but to share it after the example of our Lord Messiah: "Surely he hath borne our griefs, and carried our sorrows." (Isa. 53:4 K.J.V.) By doing that, the pastor assists a person to intensify

a capacity for suffering, enable[s] a person to "lean into the pain," to "rend the veil that lies between life and pain."[1]

A Humble Answer to "Who Am I?"

In a day like ours of New Age self-realization and be-all-you-can-be propaganda, Paul's words sound strangely alien. Yet they have the ring of reality:

"I am a person of great weakness."
"I am experienced in sinfulness."
"I am helpless and often need others."
"I carry the scars of suffering and the wounds of weakness."

Now, by way of application, it's time to take the example of Paul and, from it, ask ourselves some penetrating questions originally posed by Amy Carmichael.

Hast thou no scar?
No hidden scar on foot, or side, or hand?
I hear thee sung as mighty in the land,
I hear them hail thy bright ascendant star,
Hast thou no scar?

Hast thou no wound?
Yet I was wounded by the archers, spent,
Leaned Me against a tree to die; and rent
By ravening beasts that compassed Me, I swooned:
Hast *thou* no wound?

No wound? no scar?
Yet, as the Master shall the servant be,
And, piercèd are the feet that follow Me;
But thine are whole: can he have followed far
Who has nor wound nor scar?[2]

1. Eugene H. Peterson, *Five Smooth Stones for Pastoral Work* (Atlanta, Ga.: John Knox Press, 1980), pp. 102–3, 110.

2. Amy Carmichael, "No Scar?" in *Toward Jerusalem*. Copyright 1936 by Dohnavur Fellowship, Christian Literature Crusade—Fort Washington, Pennsylvania, and SPCK—London. Used by permission.

Living Insights

"Learning and growing" is usually a much more accurate response to "How ya doin'?" than "Fantastic!" Life's not always fantastic, but every circumstance can teach us much.

- Think back over the past year of your life. What circumstances did you face? What did God teach you through them? Use this time to express on paper how you've been learning and growing this year.

How I've Grown

_____

_____

_____

_____

_____

_____

_____

_____

_____

_____

_____

Living Insights

Is your life currently the flip side of fantastic? Or are you enjoying life right now? Either way, you probably have plenty of reason to talk to God about your life.

- Let's use our Living Insights as a time for prayer. Talk to God about your life . . . the good and the bad. Thank Him for what you can, and ask Him for His strength and wisdom for the circumstances of your life. Pray candidly, without holding back your true feelings.

Chapter 9

GLOVES OF GRACE
FOR HANDLING THORNS

2 Corinthians 12:1–10

F ew things get to us quicker than the idea that someone else is passing us up. An observant student of human nature once told this story:

> One day, the devil was traveling across the Libyan Desert. He happened upon a pack of his imps who were giving fits to a rather holy hermit, but . . . without much success. The sainted man sort of shook off all of their temptations and suggestions. Lucifer stood back only so long. And finally, after rubbing his chin and coming to certain conclusions about their approach, said to them, "What you do is too crude. Step back." And he whispered in the man of God's ear, "Your brother has just been made Bishop of Alexandria." And all of a sudden the hermit's countenance changed and a malignant presence of jealousy clouded the once serene face of the saint. "I mean, the very idea that my brother would be chosen over me." The devil looked at his demons and said, "Now that is the sort of thing I'd recommend."

We like to think we're adequate for any job that comes along, don't we? Webster says *adequate* comes from a French word that means "to make equal," similar to our phrase "equal to the task." There's a little conceit in that expression, and a hint of competition. We dislike the thought that we could be *un*equal to any challenge . . . or that someone else could be more "equal" than we are!

Types of People Who Appear Adequate

Everyone fights feelings of inadequacy. But there are three types of people whose medals make it look like they've already won the war.

The Highly Intelligent

It's easy to appear adequate when your mind is quick, when your wit is keen, and when golden phrases cascade effortlessly from your lips.

The Greatly Gifted

Some people can take lyrics and fuse them with an unforgettable melody. Others can turn a lump of clay into a dramatic sculpture. Still others can fill a blank white page with inspiring words that enlarge your heart. Their talents make them look like winners instead of warriors.

The Deeply Religious

A few people have such command of Scripture and such faith in God that they appear to glide through life with full sails and an even keel. They are so aligned with the Lord that nothing seems to pull them off course.

There's nothing wrong with being intelligent or gifted or spiritual. The problem comes when the recipients of these gifts become heroes in their own eyes.

> For who regards you as superior? And what do you have that you did not receive? But if you did receive it, why do you boast as if you had not received it? (1 Cor. 4:7)

That verse should bring us all down to size. But we face a daily temptation to glory in our own accomplishments, to puff up our chests and strut like peacocks around the yard, displaying our triumphs like gaudy feathers.

So how does God remind us to rely on His strength when He's given us such marvelous capabilities?

He reminds us of the skinny, gawky birds we are underneath those glamorous feathers. To put it as Paul did, He gives us a thorn in the flesh. Let's look at 2 Corinthians 12 to gain more insight into this significant truth.

A Classic Example: Paul

At the time of Paul's writing, Corinth has been invaded by false teachers, many with impressive credentials. Some of the people of the church there are intrigued and are beginning to be swayed by all the testimonies of great ability. So Paul, although he hates boasting, finds it necessary to remind them of his own credentials. His resumé—2 Corinthians 11—could stack up against anybody's.

However, uncomfortable with tooting his own horn, Paul adds a brief explanation of his view of boasting.

> Boasting is necessary, though it is not profitable. (12:1a)

He's implying that some boasting is horizontal—between men—and that kind of boasting is necessary on occasion. It's crucial, for instance, if you're a professor wanting potential students to know you're qualified to teach. And it's sometimes necessary in a job interview. But vertical boasting—between you and God—is never necessary. It accomplishes nothing. After all, God knows everything you've ever done and everything you're capable of.

The Corinthians need to remember that Paul is worth following. So Paul adds a postscript to his resumé, getting their attention with a credential he's never revealed before.

A Man of Unsurpassed Spiritual Ecstasy

Paul tells his readers of an experience he'd had fourteen years earlier when he was taken to Paradise.

> But I will go on to visions and revelations of the Lord. I know a man in Christ who fourteen years ago—whether in the body I do not know, or out of the body I do not know, God knows—such a man was caught up to the third heaven.[1] And I know how such a man—whether in the body or apart from the body I do not know, God knows—was caught up into Paradise, and heard inexpressible words, which a man is not permitted to speak. (vv. 1b–4)

Although Paul writes in the third person, many scholars think he is actually describing his own experience. It's possible that he chose to write this way out of modesty, or perhaps out of reverence.[2] The timing of the event places it during Paul's wilderness experience just after his conversion, a time when he was not in contact with anyone.

Imagine. Paul had actually been in the presence of the Lord, but for fourteen years he kept it to himself. Even at this writing he is reluctant to let people know about it. Unlike the media-grabbers of today, he doesn't capitalize on his experience—there's no vying for speaking engagements or contracts for magazine articles; no plans for a made-for-TV movie; no book coming out. And there's no "King

---

1. "The third heaven designates a place beyond the immediate heaven of the earth's atmosphere and beyond the further heaven of outer space and its constellations into the presence of God Himself." The NIV Study Bible (Grand Rapids, Mich.: Zondervan Bible Publishers, 1985), p. 1776.

2. For further information, see The Expositor's Bible Commentary, ed. Frank E. Gaebelein (Grand Rapids, Mich.: Zondervan Publishing House, 1976), vol. 10, p. 395.

of the Mountain" attitude. Instead of exploiting his experience, he kept it under wraps, waiting till the right time to mention it, when it might persuade some of his followers against slipping away from the truth.

A Man of Uncommon Authenticity

Far from making the most of his story-telling opportunity, Paul gives only the barest details.

> On behalf of such a man will I boast; but on my own behalf I will not boast, except in regard to my weaknesses. For if I do wish to boast I shall not be foolish, for I shall be speaking the truth; but I refrain from this, so that no one may credit me with more than he sees in me or hears from me. (vv. 5–6)

Paul wants to make sure no one gives him credit for the glory he experienced, so he doesn't describe it. Instead, he makes sure his readers know that he's telling the truth and that he refuses all temptations to boast. Why? So that no one can put him on a pedestal or canonize him into sainthood.

But Paul has a human side too. He goes on to let us see what keeps him out of the celebrity mold.

A Man of Inescapable Pain

To keep Paul from succumbing to pride, God gave him a constant reminder of his inadequacy.

> Because of the surpassing greatness of the revelations, for this reason, to keep me from exalting myself, there was given me a thorn in the flesh, a messenger of Satan to buffet me—to keep me from exalting myself! Concerning this I entreated the Lord three times that it might depart from me. (vv. 7–8)[3]

---

3. Theologians have speculated on what the "thorn" symbolizes, although Paul wasn't specific. Calvin suggested that it represents spiritual temptations—the urge for Paul to doubt and waver in his faith when things got hard. Martin Luther thought it was temptations and persecutions. Roman Catholics still believe it was sexual temptation, since Paul was celibate. Others have guessed disfigurement—such as a hunchback—or disease, like epilepsy, malarial fevers, or severe headaches. Some even speculate that it was a speech impediment. However, none of these tie in with the meaning of the word *thorn*, which means "a sharp stake"—the kind that would get under the skin and bring a pricking physical pain. For more information, see Philip Edgcumbe Hughes, *Paul's Second Epistle to the Corinthians* (Grand Rapids, Mich.: William B. Eerdmans Publishing Co., 1962), pp. 442–48.

Paul doesn't tell us what the "thorn" represents in his life. One theory, though, is that it could be failing eyesight, in light of his comments in his letter to the Galatians.

> See with what large letters I am writing to you with my own hand. (6:11)

We don't have a copy of the original manuscript, but perhaps if we did, we'd see large, scrawling letters written by Paul himself.[4] It's as if he is nearly blind and can't see well enough to write small (see also 4:15). So severe is the sting of this thorn that he pleaded with the Lord to take it away three times. But each time the request was denied. The Lord, however, didn't leave him without comfort.

A Man of Paradoxical Power

God, with a paradox, explains His response.

> And He has said to me, "My grace is sufficient for you, for power is perfected in weakness." (2 Cor. 12:9a)

The word *perfected* means "complete." It is the same word Jesus cried out as He hung on the cross: *Tetelestai!*—"It is finished!" It's over! It's complete! The reason the pain can't be removed is that it's the missing piece in power. But there is hope in the hardship— God's grace.

If only we could know, as Paul knew, when to stop asking for relief and when to submit.

> Most gladly, therefore, I will rather boast about my weaknesses, that the power of Christ may dwell in me. Therefore I am well content with weaknesses, with insults, with distresses, with persecutions, with difficulties, for Christ's sake; for when I am weak, then I am strong. (vv. 9b–10)

When Thorns Pierce Your Adequacy

Paul's life is now over and his thorn removed. But thorns like his prick our hearts as well. Yet we, too, can learn to handle these thorns with the gloves of grace.

First: *Look within.* What are the thorns that pierce your pride? Perhaps you write with a prolific pen, but arthritis for which you

---

4. Paul usually used an *amanuensis,* a secretary who wrote from Paul's dictation. See also Romans 16:22, where for the first and only time Paul's amanuensis is named in Scripture.

can find little relief grips your fingers. Or you bring others encouragement yet you can't find help to shake your own depression. Whatever your pain, whatever methods you have of dealing with it, don't view it as an enemy. Learn to greet it as a friend. That will give you joy.

Second: *Look beyond.* Instead of staring at the rose's thorns, focus on its fragrance. Remember, the thorn will give you humility, but the fragrance will give you hope.

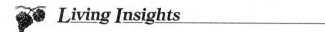 **_Living Insights_** STUDY ONE

We sometimes think of Paul as being so spiritual that he couldn't possibly relate to the struggles we face. But in 2 Corinthians 12, we see that he felt many of the same things we feel.

- Reread this chapter in a different version of the Bible. Put yourself in Paul's place and explore the emotions he must have felt. This may help you learn to respond as he did to the thorns God places in your life.

 **_Living Insights_** STUDY TWO

Just as it's difficult to find a balance between conceit and humility, sometimes it's a struggle to overcome feelings of inadequacy. Having an accurate perception of ourselves will help, but this is something we really can't do on our own.

- Get together with someone who knows you well, and ask how they perceive you. Then compare their response with how you feel about yourself. Your goal for this time should be understanding.

Chapter 10

HONESTY WRAPPED IN HUMILITY

2 Corinthians 12:7–18

Most of us remember the song made popular by America's beloved gospel singer George Beverly Shea.

> It is no secret what God can do
> What He's done for others,
> He'll do for you. . . .[1]

By changing the little three-letter word *can* to a little four-letter word *will*, we move from a simple gospel song to a deep theological fact. It is no secret what God *will* do. Even when we don't want to cooperate. Even when we resent or resist Him. Even when we forget He's there. It's no secret what God will keep on doing. And just what is that? To cause

> all things to work together for good to those who love God, those who are called according to His purpose. For whom He foreknew, He also predestined to become conformed to the image of His Son. (Rom. 8:28–29a)

What will God do? He will conform His children to the image of His Son. Or as Phillips paraphrases it: God chose us "to bear the family likeness of his Son" (v. 29a).[2]

And how does He conform us to His family likeness? By continually teaching, changing, and developing us. No day is ever wasted. No disappointment is outside His appointment. No test is ever superfluous. No surprise to us is ever a surprise to Him. He never gets off course, never forgets the game plan, never contradicts his overall purpose for us. For as Paul promises,

> He who began a good work in you will perfect it until the day of Christ Jesus. (Phil. 1:6b)

---

1. Stuart Hamblen, "It Is No Secret." © 1950 by Duchess Music Corporation.

2. J. B. Phillips, *The New Testament in Modern English*, rev. ed. (New York, N. Y.: Macmillan Publishing Co., 1972).

God, the great teacher, never runs out of ways to instruct us in this classroom of life. And with each lesson He perfects in us the image of Christ, until that day when we graduate to eternity and His task will be finally finished.

Some Methods God Employs to Teach His Children

Here are seven of the many ways God helps us become like Christ. As you read them, you may want to mentally add other ways He's working in your life.

1. By meeting our needs when we are helpless, He teaches us trust.

2. By making us wait for what we need or want, He teaches us patience.

3. By stretching us beyond the realm of the familiar, He teaches us vision.

4. By taking us through the consequences of wrong choices, He teaches us values.

5. By allowing us to fail and make terrible mistakes, He teaches us wisdom.

6. By sustaining pain and affliction, He teaches us humility.

7. By involving us in the lives of difficult people, He teaches us unselfishness.

Think back over that list. In each case, God uses the unpleasant —helplessness, waiting, mistakes, failure, pain, difficult people—to accomplish His objective. It is no secret what God is doing; He's conforming us to the image of His Son.

Today we're going to concentrate on two of the methods God used in Paul's life: pain and relationships.

The Vertical Message of Pain: Humility

In our last lesson we learned that Paul was given a "thorn in the flesh." Twice he explained why: "to keep me from exalting myself" (2 Cor. 12:7). To keep him humble, to check his spiritual pride, God had allowed this painful affliction. God didn't peer arbitrarily over the edge of heaven and say, "I think Paul needs to suffer awhile." No, He saw the possibility of spiritual conceit in the apostle and knew a thorn was needed.

It's not what the thorn *was* that mattered, but what it *did*. It made Paul into a humble servant. It forced him to rely on Christ's strength. It brought him contentment with things that normally irritate and discourage. Notice his words in verses 9–10:

> [The Lord] has said to me, "My grace is sufficient for you, for power is perfected in weakness." Most gladly, therefore, I will rather boast about my weaknesses, that the power of Christ may dwell in me. Therefore I am well content with weaknesses, with insults, with distresses, with persecutions, with difficulties, for Christ's sake; for when I am weak, then I am strong.

Three times Paul prayed for relief. Three times God answered no. Look again at Paul's response in verse 9: "Most gladly, therefore." The last time you went through a painful experience, did you say, "Most gladly, Lord, do I accept the thorn"? Or did you chafe under the experience, pleading with God to take it away. With every thorn comes a fragrance of hope—that through the thorn God teaches us the value of weakness, for in our weakness His power is displayed.

> "I asked God for strength that I might achieve.
> I was made weak that I might learn humbly to obey.
>
> I asked God for health that I might do greater things.
> I was given infirmity that I might do better things.
>
> I asked for riches that I might be happy.
> I was given poverty that I might be wise.
>
> I asked for power that I might have the praise of men.
> I was given weakness that I might feel the need of God.
>
> I asked for all things that I might enjoy life.
> I was given life that I might enjoy all things.
>
> I got nothing that I asked for
> but everything I had hoped for . . .
>
> Almost despite myself my unspoken prayers were answered.
>
> I am among all men most richly blessed."[3]

The Horizontal Test of Relationships: Unselfishness

Not only does God use pain to help us learn and grow, He also uses a horizontal test—people.

---

3. By an unknown Confederate soldier, as quoted in Tim Hansel's *When I Relax I Feel Guilty* (Elgin, Ill.: David C. Cook Publishing Co., 1979), p. 89.

In verses 11–18, Paul returns to the subject of his relationship with the Corinthians. As we've learned previously, Paul had been verbally attacked by false teachers in Corinth. And rather than defend him, the Corinthians either said nothing or agreed with them. Contrary to his style, Paul has to write back in self-defense, "foolish boasting" he calls it.

> I have become foolish; you yourselves compelled me. Actually I should have been commended by you, for in no respect was I inferior to the most eminent apostles, even though I am a nobody. The signs of a true apostle were performed among you with all perseverance, by signs and wonders and miracles. For in what respect were you treated as inferior to the rest of the churches, except that I myself did not become a burden to you? Forgive me this wrong! (vv. 11–13)

With tongue in cheek, Paul means that he had every right to expect them to provide his living expenses for preaching the gospel. But he didn't want to rely on their support, so he pleads forgiveness for this injustice he put upon them.

In spite of their lack of loyalty toward him, Paul says he wants to visit them (v. 14). Why does he want to see them again? How can he overlook their wrong treatment? Why isn't he angry and resentful? The general, underlying reason is that Paul is not a man of pride. Pride produces anger and resentment and retaliation. But Paul's thorn has replaced his pride with a spirit of humility.

Also woven into this passage are five specific reasons Paul wants to continue his relationship with the Corinthians, reasons that show evidence of a humble man.

First: *He has no image to protect.* He says in verse 11: "I am a nobody." This isn't false humility; this is how Paul views himself. And when you see yourself as nobody, you don't mind spending time with people who've taken advantage of you.

Second: *He does not keep score.* In verse 14, he says he still won't take a salary from them. They don't owe him anything.

> Here for this third time I am ready to come to you, and I will not be a burden to you; for I do not seek what is yours, but you; for children are not responsible to save up for their parents, but parents for their children.

Third: *He has a servant's heart.* He even goes a step further in verse 15.

And I will most gladly spend and be expended for your souls. If I love you the more, am I to be loved the less?

He is willing to model the example of Christ, who did not come to be ministered to but to minister, who did not come to be served but to serve, who did not come to take but to give (see Matt. 20:28). That's ministry.

Fourth: *He refuses to take unfair advantage of them.* Using exaggerated irony, Paul continues to emphasize his commitment to them.

But be that as it may, I did not burden you myself; nevertheless, crafty fellow that I am, I took you in by deceit. Certainly I have not taken advantage of you through any of those whom I have sent to you, have I? I urged Titus to go, and sent the brother with him. Titus did not take any advantage of you, did he? (2 Cor. 12:16–18a)

Paul didn't take advantage of them before, and he won't when he returns. He refuses to use them. That's why he's willing to come back and spend time with them. His slate is clean.

Fifth: *He models what he expects of others.* He concludes verse 18:

Did we not conduct ourselves in the same spirit and walk in the same steps?

The next time you feel offended or mistreated by someone, remember Paul's model of unselfishness and ask yourself a few questions.

1. Is my image a little too important to me?

2. Am I falling into the trap of keeping score?

3. Do I have a servant's heart?

4. Am I taking advantage of the other person?

5. Have I been modeling what I am expecting?

Several Ways We Can Accelerate the Learning Process

Here are three suggestions to help you apply what you're learning.

First: *Instead of reacting to pain as an enemy, remain teachable.* In the process, humility will emerge. God doesn't promise us a pain-free life, so ask Him to teach you through the pain you're experiencing.

Second: *Rather than resenting everyone because of a few who've offended you, stay involved.* As a result, unselfishness will develop.

Only when we stay involved can Christ's light shine through us to others—we can't be a witness on a deserted island.

Third: *In place of becoming offended and resentful, trust God . . .* even when He doesn't explain why. He will honor that response.

Remember, God never wastes an experience. Using both pain and people, he will continue to cultivate in us the character traits of His dear Son, Jesus Christ.

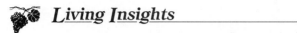 *Living Insights*

God never runs out of ways to teach us lessons, does He? This is especially evident in the passage we studied today. How many ways can you find?

• Reread 2 Corinthians 12:7–18. Using the space that follows, write down the words Paul used to describe how God taught him. Look for words like *persecutions* or *difficulties.*

Lessons God Teaches Us through Life

_____

_____

_____

_____

_____

_____

_____

_____

_____

_____

_____

_____

_____

God will continue to teach us throughout the rest of our lives. But it is possible to accelerate the learning process. We concluded this lesson with three suggestions on how to do that. In the following space, write some ways you're applying these principles in your life.

- How am I demonstrating _teachability_ through the painful experiences of my life?

_____

_____

_____

_____

_____

- It's important for me to _stay involved_ with people during tough times. What is my current involvement level?

_____

_____

_____

_____

- I should trust God, even when _why_ isn't explained. How am I applying trust these days?

_____

_____

_____

_____

Chapter 11

THREADS FOR MENDING FRAYED FEELINGS

2 Corinthians 12:19–13:4

C hristians, it is said, are a lot like porcupines. They have many good points, but they're hard to get close to. The main reason is that their prickly personalities keep needling each other with skewers of sarcasm and criticism.

Not only are individual Christians difficult to bring together, but so are their institutions. We have so many splinter groups which have parted fellowship that even the splinters have splinters. From the Church of the Way to the Church of the Better Way to the Church of the Only Way, the body of Christ has become dismembered.

No doubt about it—getting along with others, even other Christians, is no easy task. But if we are walking in fellowship with the Lord, we should be walking in fellowship with other believers as well (1 John 4:20–21). Romans 12 gives some practical advice on how to relax our quills so we can huddle closer without hurting each other.

> Be devoted to one another in brotherly love; give preference to one another in honor; not lagging behind in diligence, fervent in spirit, serving the Lord; rejoicing in hope, persevering in tribulation, devoted to prayer, contributing to the needs of the saints, practicing hospitality. Bless those who persecute you; bless and curse not. Rejoice with those who rejoice, and weep with those who weep. Be of the same mind toward one another; do not be haughty in mind, but associate with the lowly. Do not be wise in your own estimation. Never pay back evil for evil to anyone. Respect what is right in the sight of all men. If possible, so far as it depends on you, be at peace with all men. Never take your own revenge, beloved, but leave room for the wrath of God, for it is written, "Vengeance is Mine, I will repay," says the Lord. (vv. 10–19)

Does Romans 12 reflect your relationships? Are you living in peace—as far as possible—with those around you at home and at work and at church? If not, today's lesson will provide a few strands for mending the frayed feelings that have suffered the wear and tear of strained relationships.

Qualities That Encourage Relational Relief

From Eden onward the Bible is full of relationships, many of which sweep across the pages with great turbulence. Adam and Eve . . . Cain and Abel . . . Jacob and Esau . . . Joseph and his brothers . . . Samuel and Saul . . . David and Absalom . . . Paul and Barnabas are just a few of the relationships that were battered against the rocks. And calming those interpersonal storms was no easy task for those caught in the vortex.

If you're experiencing similar strain in your relationships with others, we want to suggest a few qualities that should bring some relational relief.

Insight

This is the ability to see into the mind of another, to see below the surface and discern the cause of the conflict. How good is your intuition? How good are you at looking beneath the weeds that have overgrown a relationship to unearth the root that feeds those weeds?

Honesty

This is the courage to state the truth. As Ephesians 4:15 says, we must speak the truth *in love*—but still we must speak it. Remember Nathan's honesty in confronting David (2 Sam. 12)? That's what led to the king's confession (v. 13, compare Ps. 51). It was Samuel's honesty with Saul that led to Israel's awareness of Saul's inability to reign over the nation (1 Sam. 15). And it was honesty that prompted Paul to confront Peter with his hypocrisy (Gal. 2:11–14).

Firmness

This is the resolve to stand steadfast no matter who or what is trying to move you off-center from your convictions. It's a persistence to hold your hand firmly on the rudder while riding out the storm.

Clarity

This is the skill to work through conflicts by communicating what the issues are and where the misunderstandings lie.

With these four qualities in mind, we come to our passage for today: 2 Corinthians 12:19–13:4.

Background on the Paul-Corinthian Conflict

Both letters to the Corinthians are needed to clarify the conflict mentioned in this passage. The conflict was from both outside and inside the church.

From without, there were distinct cultural differences. Paul was Jewish; the Corinthians were Greeks. Paul was intellectual; the Corinthians were emotional. Paul was theological; the Corinthians were rational. Added to these external conflicts were the false teachers. They undermined the content of Paul's teaching, his teaching credentials, and even his character.

From within the church, there was the problem of the Corinthians comparing Paul to Peter and Apollos, which resulted in the formation of cliques (1 Cor. 1:10–12). There were also the problems of carnality (3:1–9) and immorality (5:1–13). Some even accused the apostle of hypocrisy (2 Cor. 10:10).

So it was no little tiff. The friction had been heated for some time. It's interesting to note that when we analyze Paul's approach to cooling this conflict, he employs all four of the qualities we mentioned earlier—insight, honesty, firmness, and clarity.

Exposing Wrong and Healing a Rift

In 2 Corinthians 12:19, Paul reveals insight by *addressing the unspoken.*

> All this time you have been thinking that we are defending ourselves to you. Actually, it is in the sight of God that we have been speaking in Christ; and all for your upbuilding, beloved.

First, he states their thinking. Second, he declares his credibility in the sight of God. Third, he states his motive in doing all things for their edification.

In verses 20–21, Paul models honesty by *admitting the unpleasant.*

> For I am afraid that perhaps when I come I may find you to be not what I wish and may be found by you to be not what you wish; that perhaps there may be strife, jealousy, angry tempers, disputes, slanders, gossip, arrogance, disturbances. (v. 20)

The first unpleasant thing Paul mentions is *strife*—a word for battle, discord, and arguments. Second in the list is *jealousy.* Jealousy is wanting to keep what you already have, as opposed to envy, which wants to have what someone else keeps. Next he lists *angry tempers*—sudden explosions or outbursts of anger. *Disputes* are the bitter fruit of a factious spirit and a negative, rigid, and caustic mind-set. *Slanders* are loud-mouthed attacks in public. *Gossip*, on the other hand, is more insidious, lurking behind the back, in the shadows of respectability. Both, however, are aimed at character assassination. *Arrogance* is pride or conceit, exalting oneself over another. The final word in verse 20 is *disturbances*, which denotes tumult and anarchy.

Besides these sins of the heart and tongue, the Corinthians were also known for their sins of the body.

> I am afraid that when I come again my God may
> humiliate me before you, and I may mourn over many
> of those who have sinned in the past and not repented
> of the impurity, immorality and sensuality which they
> have practiced. (v. 21)

The very word *Corinthian* was a synonym for moral debauchery. In fact, to *Corinthianize* meant "to fornicate."

The three qualities in verse 21 form a downward spiral—from *impurity*, a general word for uncleanness, to *immorality*, which includes fornication and adultery, down to *sensuality*, a word describing wanton insolence that is devoid of shame.

It was no surprise to Paul that Corinth was a seething cauldron of conflict and immorality. However, when those things spilled over into the church, he fell on his face in shame and sadness.

May we get painfully personal for a moment? Has the world squeezed you into its mold? Or are you remolding the world? Are you living the lifestyle of the carnal Corinthians? Or are you incarnating the character of Christ? Remember: If you are not salt infiltrating a decaying world, the decaying world is infiltrating you.

As we come to chapter 13, we see Paul's firmness in *warning the unrepentant.*

> This is the third time I am coming to you. Every fact
> is to be confirmed by the testimony of two or three
> witnesses. (v. 1)

First, in appealing to the Law, Paul states that he is through warning them; discipline is imminent. Second, by affirming his return, he promises a basement-to-attic housecleaning.

> I have previously said when present the second time,
> and though now absent I say in advance to those who

have sinned in the past and to all the rest as well, that if I come again, I will not spare anyone. (v. 2)

Paul is exhorting them to clean up their lives, because when he comes, he's going to give their lifestyles the white-glove test. He will open every cupboard, run his fingers over every shelf, and peer into every nook and cranny of their lives.

There comes a time in the medical field when prescriptions fail to solve the patient's problems. That's when surgery must be considered, when the patient must submit to the knife. And that's precisely what Paul is telling them—"If my prescription hasn't worked by the time I come, then get ready for major surgery." It is this type of firmness that gave credibility to all Paul's other attributes.

Finally, Paul demonstrates his clear-headed logic by *explaining the unclear.*

> Since you are seeking for proof of the Christ who speaks in me, and who is not weak toward you, but mighty in you. For indeed He was crucified because of weakness, yet He lives because of the power of God. For we also are weak in Him, yet we shall live with Him because of the power of God directed toward you. (vv. 3–4)

The Corinthians had criticized Paul for coming off strong in his letters but weak in his appearance because he was not especially authoritative or assertive. His gentle demeanor raised doubts about his claim to apostolic power and authority. He explains that his impending severity would erase all misguided judgment. When he came, they would have no further question regarding his authority.

It seems a shame that adults, especially Christian adults, should ever need to be treated like children. But that was their level of spiritual maturity at the time (1 Cor. 3:1–2). Paul had to be firm with them as a parent would toward a wayward child (Heb. 12:5–13).

Could it be that every evidence of rebellion and immorality can be traced back to a stubborn streak that was not dealt with firmly enough or decisively enough in our childhood? Examine for a moment the areas of your life that are causing turmoil. How far back can you find traces of rebellion in your life? Like a tenaciously stubborn root, these problems often lie deep within us. And no matter how often we cut the weeds on the surface, that won't bring lasting peace because the problem is deeper than that.

The Next Time You Face a Conflict

Conflicts will crop up in your life as sure as weeds in a garden. When they do, here are three pieces of advice that will help you hoe them out of your life.

First: *Before blaming, attempt identification.* Put yourself in the other person's place, as Paul did when he told them what they were thinking. It's amazing what that perspective will do when a conflict arises.

Second: *Instead of arguing, ask some questions:* What is the root of this? Is my motive pure? Do I seek peace? Am I being totally honest? Am I overlooking my part of the conflict? Do both of us really desire a resolution of the conflict?

Third: *Rather than retaliating, pursue restoration.* Remember the verse in Romans?

> If possible, so far as it depends on you, be at peace with all men. (12:18)

There's a wonderful truth in Galatians 6:1 that speaks to this whole issue of restoration.

> Brothers, if someone is caught in a sin, you who are spiritual should restore him gently. (NIV)

The word *restore* is from the Greek word *katartizō*. It's used to describe the mending of a torn net, the restoring of military forces by feeding or equipping them, and the setting of a bone that is broken or out of joint.

That was exactly Paul's task in coming to Corinth—to restore the broken bone of fractured fellowship. He rises to the occasion with all the qualities of a great surgeon who has a gentle yet firm hand. Love that is tender. Love that is tough. And, in restoring, he sets a wonderful example for how we, too, should handle conflict in our relationships with others.

Living Insights

The Word of God is so practical! It is chock-full of relationships and the tensions that come with them. This fact helps us see biblical characters as real people, not larger than life.

- Let's examine some of the human relationships in Scripture. Choose one or several of the following relationships to explore.

Look for strengths, weaknesses, struggles, and solutions, and write your observations in the space that follows.

Adam and Eve	Saul and David
Cain and Abel	Absalom and David
Jacob and Esau	Paul and Barnabas
Joseph and his brothers	Peter and Paul
Samuel and Saul	The apostle John and Diotrephes

Observing Biblical Relationships

_____

_____

_____

_____

_____

_____

_____

_____

_____

_____

_____

_____

Living Insights   STUDY TWO

As you read and studied about frayed feelings, was the message hitting close to home? Are there hurts in your life that are in need of mending? Let's make an attempt at dealing with these issues.

• Is there something you can do to mend some frayed feelings? Can you initiate some sort of communication to bring healing? Write a note, place a call, or make a visit, and in doing so, take a few strides toward healing a hurt.

Chapter 12

PASSING THE FAITH TEST
2 Corinthians 13:5–10

S ocrates once said, "The unexamined life is not worth living."[1] Yet how few of us really search ourselves. How rarely in the busy traffic of life do we ever step on the brakes, pull to the side of the road, pop the hood, and study the condition of our souls. How often do we test the fluid levels that prevent us from becoming dry, or the electrical system that keeps us charged up?

All of this becomes extremely practical when we come to Paul's teaching in 2 Corinthians 13:5–10. These verses offer some of the most searching exhortations in the New Testament, calling on Christians to examine their lives to see if indeed they are "in the faith."

A Test That Many Never Take

From pop tests to blood tests, and from bar exams to eye exams, testing is a regular part of life. Aside from medical, academic, and professional tests, there are personal tests that we all must face: sickness, affliction, broken dreams, failures, peer pressure, moral temptation. But there is one test many of us never take, a test found in 2 Corinthians 13:5.

> Test yourselves to see if you are in the faith; examine yourselves! Or do you not recognize this about yourselves, that Jesus Christ is in you—unless indeed you fail the test?

Underscore the word *yourselves*. It occurs three times in this verse. Not only is the term emphasized by repetition, it is emphasized in Greek by being placed out of the normal order of the sentence structure. A more literal rendering might read: "You yourselves test . . . you yourselves prove . . . that Jesus Christ is in you." The emphasis is on each one of us examining ourselves to see whether Jesus is, in reality, in us. The test doesn't ask how faithful we are in church attendance, how well we say mealtime prayers, or how many verses of the Bible we've memorized. It skips to the bottom line, to the most rudimentary of questions regarding whether we stand in the circle of faith of which Christ is the center.

---

1. Socrates, in *The Dialogues of Plato*, trans. Benjamin Jowett, in *Great Books of the Western World* (Chicago, Ill.: Encyclopaedia Britannica, 1952), vol. 7, p. 210.

An examination calls for three things: a test—*peirazō*—translated simply "test"; a proof—*dokimazō*—translated "examine"; and a perception—*epiginōskō*—translated "to recognize." These three terms guide us in conducting a self-examination of our faith.

First: *Give yourself an objective test.* Ask yourself: Do I have a personal relationship with Christ? Have I experienced any significant changes in my life through knowing Him? Do I experience His leading, His presence, His peace, His joy?

Second: *Call to mind specific proof that you're a Christian.* The term *dokimazō* carries with it the idea of examining for the purpose of approving, not failing. Can you show evidence that you are really a changed person? How different are your thoughts? Your habits? Your goals? Your relationships? Your feelings?

Third: *Ask yourself if you have an inner discernment.* Are you growing in knowledge, confidence, and peace? Or are you more often in a quandary, full of unsettling questions, doubts, and uncertainties?

In verse 6, Paul turns the finger he's pointed at them back on himself.

> But I trust that you will realize that we ourselves do
> not fail the test.

Before we ever examine another person's life, we should look first to ourselves. In fact, self-examination is encouraged in Scripture far more than the examination of others.

> "Do not judge lest you be judged. For in the way you
> judge, you will be judged; and by your standard of
> measure, it will be measured to you. And why do you
> look at the speck that is in your brother's eye, but do
> not notice the log that is in your own eye? Or how
> can you say to your brother, 'Let me take the speck
> out of your eye,' and behold, the log is in your own
> eye? You hypocrite, first take the log out of your own
> eye, and then you will see clearly to take the speck
> out of your brother's eye." (Matt. 7:1–5)

This doesn't mean we never examine critically another person's life, for later in that same sermon Jesus says:

> "Beware of the false prophets, who come to you in
> sheep's clothing, but inwardly are ravenous wolves.
> You will know them by their fruits. Grapes are not
> gathered from thorn bushes, nor figs from thistles, are
> they? Even so, every good tree bears good fruit; but

the bad tree bears bad fruit. A good tree cannot produce bad fruit, nor can a bad tree produce good fruit. Every tree that does not bear good fruit is cut down and thrown into the fire. So then, you will know them by their fruits. (vv. 15–20)

Although we are not to nitpick the fabric of people's faith, we are called to examine the fruit in their lives. We are called to look with a surgeon's eye upon those who have made some moral break with the faith. Yet all the while we must look with compassion and with a view toward gently restoring them, looking also at ourselves lest we be tempted to think we're better than they are (Gal. 6:1; compare 5:25).

Through what kind of eyes—critical or compassionate—do you see others? When you confront people, is it to expose them or to restore them? If you take even the slightest delight in the confrontation, you have the wrong motivation.

Verse 7 of 2 Corinthians 13 is reminiscent of words parents say to children.

Now we pray to God that you do no wrong; not that we ourselves may appear approved, but that you may do what is right, even though we should appear unapproved.

In this verse, Paul views his reputation as secondary, even inconsequential, to theirs. He's concerned that his students learn, not that he gains the reputation of being a good teacher. It's for their sake, not his, that he hopes they pass the test. By way of application, when you give yourself this test and take a good hard look at your life, it's not to make your pastor look good; it's so you will pass and stand approved in your own eyes.

Like all good teachers, Paul is committed to the pursuit of truth. And he's convinced that truth will ultimately win out.

For we can do nothing against the truth, but only for the truth. (v. 8)

Paul is like so many parents who beam with delight at their emerging adolescent children, glorying in the fact that although they themselves are growing older and weaker, the children are growing up and growing stronger.

For we rejoice when we ourselves are weak but you are strong; this we also pray for, that you be made complete. (v. 9)

Appealing to his apostolic authority, Paul reiterates the intention of his letter.

> For this reason I am writing these things while absent, in order that when present I may not use severity, in accordance with the authority which the Lord gave me, for building up and not for tearing down. (v. 10)

In many churches and organizations, leaders are feared. Submission is hammered into people's heads, and accountability is rigid and oppressive. Now there's nothing wrong with accountability, but there is something terribly wrong when it's forced.

First Peter 5:1–3 gives the guidelines on how authority should be handled in the church by its leaders.

> Therefore, I exhort the elders among you, as your fellow elder and witness of the sufferings of Christ, and a partaker also of the glory that is to be revealed, shepherd the flock of God among you, exercising oversight not under compulsion, but voluntarily, according to the will of God; and not for sordid gain, but with eagerness; nor yet as lording it over those allotted to your charge, but proving to be examples to the flock.

There's an absence of fear in this type of leadership, and an absence of pride. The image is one of leading sheep, not driving cattle. There is no compulsion in the shepherd and no coercion of the sheep.

While Peter articulates warnings regarding church leadership, John shows us an example of a leader run amuck.

> I wrote something to the church; but Diotrephes, who loves to be first among them, does not accept what we say. For this reason, if I come, I will call attention to his deeds which he does, unjustly accusing us with wicked words; and not satisfied with this, neither does he himself receive the brethren, and he forbids those who desire to do so, and puts them out of the church. (3 John 9–10)

When a person in leadership rules dictatorially and enlarges his earthly authority, the lordship of Jesus Christ is eclipsed.

A Suggested Process for Taking the Test

There are three primary benefits to self-testing. One, it reveals the truth to us, which is what will ultimately set us free (John 8:32).

Two, it keeps us from a hypercritical attitude. Three, it removes a lot of debris that can clog our lives and stagnate the fresh flow of energy.

Since the benefits for testing ourselves are so positive, let's sharpen our pencils and get down to business. Here are a few suggestions to keep in mind.

1. *Ask the hard questions.* We take tests to find out where we are and how much we've learned. In the same way, asking yourself the following questions will help you find out where you are in your relationship with God, and how that relationship affects your life.

   - Does Christ really live in me?

   - Are there any evidences of change in my life?

   - Am I getting easier to live with?

   - Are my attitudes any different now than they were in the past?

   - If I were to die tonight, would Christ meet me with open arms?

2. *Answer honestly.* Remember, God knows your heart, but have you ever taken the time to find out where you stand? The answers to these questions have eternal consequences, so be truthful with yourself.

3. *Review your answers.* If you answered no to any questions, find out why. Then make plans to correct those areas. If you answered yes, prove your answers with your life. Make that fruit available for everyone to see and to touch and to taste.

4. *Resist the temptation to rationalize.* Don't succumb to blaming your childhood, your mate, your job, your circumstances for keeping you from growing spiritually. All of those things certainly affect your life, but you don't have to be stuck in a puddle of despair. Let God work with you right where you are . . . allow Him to create in you a clean heart and a righteous spirit (Ps. 51:10).

Monday	**May 22**	**Not All "Ministries" Are Ministries** 2 Corinthians 11:1–15
Tuesday	**May 23**	**Not All "Ministries" Are Ministries**
Wednesday	**May 24**	**The Flip Side of "Fantastic"** 2 Corinthians 11:16–33
Thursday	**May 25**	**The Flip Side of "Fantastic"**
Friday	**May 26**	**Gloves of Grace for Handling Thorns** 2 Corinthians 12:1–10
Monday	**May 29**	**Gloves of Grace for Handling Thorns**
Tuesday	**May 30**	**Honesty Wrapped in Humility** 2 Corinthians 12:7–18
Wednesday	**May 31**	**Honesty Wrapped in Humility**
Thursday	**June 1**	**Threads for Mending Frayed Feelings** 2 Corinthians 12:19–13:4
Friday	**June 2**	**Threads for Mending Frayed Feelings**
Monday	**June 5**	**Passing the Faith Test** 2 Corinthians 13:5–10
Tuesday	**June 6**	**Passing the Faith Test**
Wednesday	**June 7**	**A Love Letter, Sealed with a Kiss** 2 Corinthians 13:11–14
Thursday	**June 8**	**A Love Letter, Sealed with a Kiss**
Friday	**June 9**	**Heart Trouble** Isaiah 29:13–16, Matthew 15:1–20
Monday	**June 12**	**Heart Trouble**

INSIGHT FOR LIVING

Broadcast Schedule

May 4–June 12, 1989

A Minister Everyone Would Respect
A Study of 2 Corinthians 8–13

Thursday	**May 4**	**Making Good Sense with Our Dollars** 2 Corinthians 8:1–9
Friday	**May 5**	**Making Good Sense with Our Dollars**
Monday	**May 8**	**Fanning the Financial Fire** 2 Corinthians 8:10–24
Tuesday	**May 9**	**Fanning the Financial Fire**
Wednesday	**May 10**	**The Trip to Bountiful Giving** 2 Corinthians 9:1–6
Thursday	**May 11**	**The Trip to Bountiful Giving**
Friday	**May 12**	**Giving by Grace** 2 Corinthians 9:6–15
Monday	**May 15**	**Giving by Grace**
Tuesday	**May 16**	**A Bloodless Battle Nobody Notices** 2 Corinthians 10:1–6
Wednesday	**May 17**	**A Bloodless Battle Nobody Notices**
Thursday	**May 18**	**Stabilized Though Criticized** 2 Corinthians 10:7–18
Friday	**May 19**	**Stabilized Though Criticized**

Faith . . . unquestionably one of the key words in all of Scripture. As we come to this final chapter in 2 Corinthians, let's take one last look at some other key words in this chapter.

- Reread 2 Corinthians 13:5–10 and find eight or ten key words in the text. Write out the meaning of each word, using a Bible dictionary if necessary. Then jot down a sentence on the significance of the word to the passage.

2 Corinthians 13:5–10

Key word: _____

Meaning: _____

_____

Significance: _____

_____

Key word: _____

Meaning: _____

_____

Significance: _____

_____

Key word: _____

Meaning: _____

_____

Significance: _____

_____

Key word: _____

Meaning: _____

_____

Significance: _____

_____

Key word: _____

Meaning: _____

_____

Significance: _____

_____

Key word: _____

Meaning: _____

_____

Significance: _____

_____

Key word: _____

Meaning: _____

_____

Significance: _____

_____

Key word: _____

Meaning: _____

_____

Significance: _____

_____

Key word: _____

Meaning: _____

_____

Significance: _____

_____

Key word: _____

Meaning: _____

_____

Significance: _____

_____

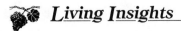 **Living Insights** STUDY TWO

Has this series been of value to you? If so, the credit really goes to the Lord, our great teacher. Let's pause for a few minutes to thank Him for the wonderful lessons He's given us in the passages we've studied.

- Is there something specific for which you can thank God today? Did He teach you an important lesson or two through these studies? Lift up your prayers of praise and thanksgiving to Him. There's no better use of our Living Insights than to honor the Source of Truth.

Chapter 13

A LOVE LETTER, SEALED WITH A KISS

2 Corinthians 13:11–14

An old Russian proverb goes like this:

> It is the same with people as it is with donkeys: whoever would hold them fast must get a very good grip on their ears.

So it has been with our study of the latter half of 2 Corinthians. Paul has got a very good grip on the Corinthians' ears, and on our ears as well. Our attention has been held fast as we've seen the incredible relevance of Paul's first-century words to our twentieth-century lives.

Discussing such subjects as giving, grace, spiritual warfare, relationships, cults, suffering, God's sufficiency, and faith, Paul has enlightened, instructed, indicted, and encouraged. And in every passage he's affirmed his love for this body of believers.

Before we approach the final four words of this letter of love, let's look back at where we've been.

An Encouraging Glance at the Truth Behind Us

Sandwiched between a brief introduction (1:1–2) and an equally brief conclusion (13:11–14) is the meat of 2 Corinthians, which can be divided into three parts.

In chapters 1–7, Paul deals with some crucial concerns—suffering, ministry, and godliness.[1] Then in chapters 8–9 he discusses grace giving, exhorting his readers to put their treasure where their heart is. And finally, in chapters 10–13, he presents his apostolic credentials, reluctantly responding to the critics who denied his authority.

Looking back at these sections, we can learn four principles that will summarize what this letter is all about.

---

1. Second Corinthians 1–7 is covered in the study guide *A Ministry Anyone Could Trust,* coauthored by Ken Gire, from the Bible-teaching ministry of Charles R. Swindoll (Fullerton, Calif.: Insight for Living, 1989).

First: *Great people are not immune to hard times.* In 4:7–18 and 1:8–10, Paul teaches us that hard times are like God's anvil, where He shapes us into the likeness of His Son. Right now, you may be feeling the flames of the furnace, wondering why you have to submit to the pain of being reshaped. But such difficult times will be the making of greatness if you'll let God carry out His plan (4:17–18). This leads directly to our next principle.

Second: *Hard times bring tensions that may seem confusing.* It just doesn't seem fair to have to struggle—especially when we've been walking with God. In fact, it seems to contradict His love. Why does the Christian life have to include afflictions, hardships, and distresses, as well as purity, knowledge, and patience (6:4b, 6a)? Why do we have to experience the contrasts of "glory and dishonor, . . . evil report and good report; regarded as deceivers and yet true" (v. 8)? This paradox points to the third principle.

Third: *Such confusion is a needed reminder of our humanity.* Chapter 12 reminds us that God's grace penetrates the confusing fog of our weakness, allowing the power of Jesus Christ to shine through (vv. 9–10). God uses our limited humanity—our failures, our hurts, our pain—to show His limitless deity.

Fourth: *Difficulty plus humanity equals humility and maturity.* You'll never meet a humble person who hasn't hurt, nor a mature person who hasn't known trials. Never. Paul called himself "a nobody" (12:11), but he manifested the maturity of "a true apostle" (v. 12). Unless we submit to the blows and buffeting and pain that God allows, we won't grow up. We'll be overgrown children, playing in the streets of carnality.

A Concluding Look at Second Corinthians

As we turn to today's passage in 13:11–14, we first see that Paul qualifies his closing remarks. "Finally, brethren," he says in verse 11, meaning that his following words are just for believers, Corinthian as well as current.

Some Practical Commands

Paul gives six practical commands in verses 11–12 for how we are to conduct our lives.

> Finally, brethren, rejoice, be made complete, be comforted, be like-minded, live in peace; and the God of love and peace shall be with you. Greet one another with a holy kiss.

Let's take a closer look at each command.

Rejoice. Some translations render this "farewell" or "good-bye," but the root term is "be joyful." In other words, laugh more—let laughter spill from your life, filling the walls of your home and your workplace. Scientists have discovered that laughter even has medical benefits—it creates morphinelike endoenzymes in the brain that actually reduce pain.[2] Solomon also knew the benefits of laughter when he wrote, "A joyful heart is good medicine, / But a broken spirit dries up the bones" (Prov. 17:22).

Be made complete. This comes from the Greek word *katartizō,* which means "restoration," and has in mind supplying what is missing to bring about full usefulness. It's used for mending a torn net, setting a broken bone, equipping an army with supplies, or patching up anything that has been injured or damaged. The Revised Standard Version translates this phrase, "Mend your ways," an excellent exhortation for all of us. Have you mended your ways after being confronted with the truths in 2 Corinthians? Have you been restored? What difference have these studies made in your life? It's not important how many books of the Bible we get through, but how many books get through us.

Be comforted. The Greek term Paul uses here, *parakaleō,* has varied meanings. It's the same word John uses for the Holy Spirit, who comes alongside to help us. It can also be a command—to encourage, cheer, or console one another. But many scholars believe Paul is using it in the sense of exhortation. For example, Philip Edgcumbe Hughes says, "It seems preferable to translate it here in its other sense, namely, 'be admonished' or 'heed my appeal' (RSV)[3] —that is, respond to the plea which this epistle conveys."[4] Carried a step further, we can find comfort in following Paul's advice, in getting our lives in order.

Be like-minded. Paul literally wrote, "Think the same thing." Now he's not asking for uniformity in dress or appearance or actions. He's asking all of us to have the same focus. In his letter to the church at Philippi, he stresses this same command.

> Make my joy complete by being of the same mind,
> maintaining the same love, united in spirit, intent on

2. Bruce Larson, *There's a Lot More to Health than Not Being Sick* (Waco, Tex.: Word Books, 1981), p. 124.

3. The NIV renders it "listen to my appeal."

4. Philip Edgcumbe Hughes, *Paul's Second Epistle to the Corinthians* (Grand Rapids, Mich.: William B. Eerdmans Publishing Co., 1962), p. 487.

one purpose. Do nothing from selfishness or empty conceit, but with humility of mind let each of you regard one another as more important than himself; do not merely look out for your own personal interests, but also for the interests of others. Have this attitude in yourselves which was also in Christ Jesus. (Phil. 2:2–5)

When we are like-minded toward Christ, we are also like-minded toward others, unselfish and open and supportive. That is the secret of close relationships.

Live in peace. This was Paul's goal for the churches—that they stay together, peacefully. Who wants to belong to an organization whose members can't get along? We are to be different from the world, not selfishly pushing our way to the top, but working together harmoniously. Look at your own life right now. Do you live in peace? Do you calm the waters? Or do you like to stir things up? Are you a friend, or an adversary?

Greet one another with a holy kiss. Paul is merely telling the Corinthians to be affectionate with each other. Not from impure or sensual motives, but from holiness and brotherly love. The early believers were known for their visible expressions of love. But later the affection grew more formal, and by 1250 Archbishop Walter in England introduced a pax—a board that had been kissed by the clergy and was then passed among the congregation to be kissed. Where's the warmth in that? God didn't want us to greet each other with a holy board, but with a holy kiss.

Reminders Worth Remembering

Paul leaves two wonderful promises with the Corinthians.

The God of love and peace shall be with you. . . . All the saints greet you. (2 Cor. 13:11b, 13)

First: *We can count on divine presence.* God will be with us. And second: *We can also count on earthly companionship.* We are joined together in family with all of our Christian brothers and sisters.

Two Tips on Making the Message Stay with Us

We've learned so much from 2 Corinthians that it's hard for our minds to retain it all. But two tips will help reinforce Paul's overall message.

First: *Release the love of God, wherever you may be.* Paul did that with the Corinthians, tugging their wayward hearts back to God. There's nothing more magnetic than God's love.

Second: *Remember the God of love, whatever may happen to you.*
God is there with you in all your struggles and all your pain. He
loves you with such incredible depth that He gave His Son so that
you might spend eternity with Him. It's easy to remember Him when
everything's going great. But if you can remember His love when
darkness overcomes you, the message of 2 Corinthians will have
gone through you.

We can't improve upon Paul's conclusion, the timeless benediction used by the church ever since he first penned it:

> The grace of the Lord Jesus Christ, and the love of
> God, and the fellowship of the Holy Spirit, be with
> you all. (v. 14)

 Living Insights

As Paul closes his letter, he gives us some helpful advice for
living out the rest of our days. Among other things, we are exhorted
to rejoice, be comforted, be like-minded, and live in peace. Let's
take a closer look at these admonitions.

* With the help of a concordance, conduct a Scripture search on
one of these four words: *rejoice, comfort, like-minded, peace.* Circle
the word you want to research, and record your findings below,
along with your summary of the key verses.

Scripture Search

References	Summary Statements
_____	_____
	_____
_____	_____
	_____
_____	_____
	_____
_____	_____

_____   _____

                    _____

_____   _____

                    _____

_____   _____

                    _____

_____   _____

                    _____

_____   _____

                    _____

                    _____

 Living Insights _____ STUDY TWO

Are you experiencing difficulty and disillusionment in some area of your life? Maybe it has to do with a relationship, a job, finances, health, or even self-image. Do you feel forsaken by God? Have you forgotten what it feels like to be really happy?

If so, turn to Lamentations 3, where Jeremiah, the prophet of God, experienced similar feelings. Verses 1–20 focus on the disillusionment the prophet was going through. But his emotions take a turn for the better in verses 21–32 as he focuses on the great attributes of God—His lovingkindness, His compassion, and His faithfulness.

Meditate on verses 21–32, and apply them to your present circumstances. Then use those personalized verses as your prayer list, and see if that doesn't help you get a better perspective on your problems.

Chapter 14

HEART TROUBLE
Isaiah 29:13–16, Matthew 15:1–20

T he heart is the most vital of all our organs, for it gives life to every cell in our body. Every day, the heart beats over one hundred thousand times, sending oxygen and nutrition through one hundred thousand miles of arteries, veins, and capillaries. In fact, the heart does enough work in just one hour to lift a five-ton weight more than a foot off the ground. All this from a muscle no bigger than our fist.

God says a lot about the heart. If we were to look up the word in an exhaustive concordance, we would find more than a thousand references. Isn't it interesting that God chooses a term so vital to physical life when referring to our spiritual life? Using phrases like "a heart of integrity" . . . "a heart of compassion" . . . "a joyful heart," He describes a healthy spiritual life. And with phrases like a "hardened heart" . . . "a divided heart" . . . "a proud heart," He describes an unhealthy one.

Heart disease is the number-one killer in the United States. The sad thing about that statistic is that with proper diet and exercise, most of those deaths could have been prevented. Heart trouble is also the number-one killer regarding our spiritual lives. That's why Solomon says in Proverbs 4:23:

> Watch over your heart with all diligence,
> For from it flow the springs of life.

Biblical Usage

Biblically, the term *heart* represents our whole inner being. This is how the word is used in 1 Samuel 16:7.

> The Lord said to Samuel, "Do not look at his appearance or at the height of his stature, because I have rejected him; for God sees not as man sees, for man looks at the outward appearance, but the Lord looks at the heart."

This message was not a part of the original series but is compatible with it.

In Hebrew, the word for "heart" is *lebab*. It "not only includes the motives, feelings, affections, and desires, but also the will, the aims, the principles, the thoughts, and the intellect."[1]

The Greek word for "heart" is *kardia*, from which we get the word *cardiology*. Gerhard Kittel, in his massive, nine-volume work on New Testament words, describes the term as follows:

> The heart is the centre of the inner life of man and the source or seat of all the forces and functions of soul and spirit. . . . Thus [*kardia*] comes to stand for the whole of the inner being of man in contrast to his external side. . . . Thus the heart is supremely the one centre in man to which God turns, in which the religious life is rooted, which determines moral conduct.[2]

In our lesson today, we're going to use as scalpels a passage from the Old Testament and one from the New to perform a little open-heart surgery.

> For the word of God is living and active and sharper than any two-edged sword, and piercing as far as the division of soul and spirit, of both joints and marrow, and able to judge the thoughts and intentions of the heart. (Heb. 4:12)

Old Testament Passage

The Lord gave the prophet Isaiah a vision of woe concerning Jerusalem (see Isa. 28–33). Isaiah's assignment was to speak publicly about that vision. In 29:13 he begins with a spiritual diagnosis after placing a stethoscope on the city's chest.

> Then the Lord said,
> "Because this people draw near with their words
> And honor Me with their lip service,
> But they remove their hearts far from Me,
> And their reverence for Me consists of tradition
>   learned by rote."

Most likely, this is a reference to prayer, where the people were going through the motions of formal prayer without engaging their

1. Robert Baker Girdlestone, *Synonyms of the Old Testament* (1897; reproduction, Grand Rapids, Mich.: William B. Eerdmans Publishing Co., n.d.), p. 65.

2. Gerhard Kittel, ed., *Theological Dictionary of the New Testament,* trans. Geoffrey W. Bromiley (Grand Rapids, Mich.: William B. Eerdmans Publishing Co., 1965), vol. 3, pp. 611–12.

hearts. But God is not impressed with empty motions, no matter how eloquent (Matt. 6:5–7). This is the first symptom of heart trouble—the spiritual life becomes routine and external. The second spiritual symptom is found in Isaiah 29:15.

> Woe to those who deeply hide their plans from the
> Lord,
> And whose deeds are done in a dark place,
> And they say, "Who sees us?" or "Who knows us?"

This is a picture of people living apart from God, distant from any life-changing contact with Him. No matter how active, the life lived apart from a vital relationship with God is unfruitful (John 15:5).

This independence from God stems from a theological error. And in pointing out this problem, the prophet moves from examining the people's symptoms to diagnosing their disease.

> You turn things around!
> Shall the potter be considered as equal with the clay,
> That what is made should say to its maker, "He did
> not make me";
> Or what is formed say to him who formed it, "He has
> no understanding"? (Isa. 29:16)

The people saw God as their equal, of little more concern to them than just another person. As a result, they felt they could do whatever they pleased without suffering any consequences. They failed to realize that like the potter, who is sovereign over the clay, so God has complete dominion over their lives. Nothing could be hidden from such a God—not even the innermost recesses of their hearts (Ps. 139).

New Testament Passage

Just as physical heart trouble is often hereditary, so spiritual heart disease is often passed from generation to generation. And just as this disease afflicted the Old Testament Jews, so it was the number-one killer of spiritual life at the time of Christ.

In Matthew 15, Jesus describes the lives of some extremely important religious leaders who looked holy on the outside but who were hypocrites underneath. Verses 1–6 demonstrate that *when your heart is far from God, you care more about external tradition than about God's revelation.*

> Then some Pharisees and scribes came to Jesus from
> Jerusalem, saying, "Why do Your disciples transgress
> the tradition of the elders? For they do not wash their

hands when they eat bread." And He answered and said to them, "And why do you yourselves transgress the commandment of God for the sake of your tradition? For God said, 'Honor your father and mother,' and, 'He who speaks evil of father or mother, let him be put to death.' But you say, 'Whoever shall say to his father or mother, "Anything of mine you might have been helped by has been given to God," he is not to honor his father or his mother.' And thus you invalidated the word of God for the sake of your tradition." (vv. 1–6)

The word *invalidated* in verse 6 comes from the Greek root *kuros*, which means "authority." Here the term is *akuroō*, meaning "non-authority." Jesus is saying that when they exalt their traditions, placing them on equal footing with Scripture, they take away the true authority of divine revelation.

Verses 7–9 demonstrate another principle: *When your heart is diseased, you practice hypocrisy rather than model authenticity.*

"You hypocrites, rightly did Isaiah prophesy of you, saying,
'This people honors Me with their lips,
But their heart is far away from Me.
But in vain do they worship Me,
Teaching as doctrines the precepts of men.' "

Those verses sound familiar? That's because they're from the passage in Isaiah we looked at earlier (29:13).

Notice that the religious leaders' problem was not worship trouble or doctrinal trouble, but *heart* trouble. For the heart is a Pandora's box of all kinds of evil.

And after He called the multitude to Him, He said to them, "Hear, and understand. Not what enters into the mouth defiles the man, but what proceeds out of the mouth, this defiles the man. . . . But the things that proceed out of the mouth come from the heart, and those defile the man. For out of the heart come evil thoughts, murders, adulteries, fornications, thefts, false witness, slanders. These are the things which defile the man; but to eat with unwashed hands does not defile the man." (Matt. 15:10–11, 18–20)

Concluding Applications

Just as a cardiologist would ask you to fill out your medical history during a visit, so we would like you to take a few minutes to answer the following questions about your spiritual condition.

Question	*Circle Answer*	
Has worship become dry and overly formal?	Yes	No
Is prayer a series of meaningless words for you?	Yes	No
Does God seem distant?	Yes	No
Have you wondered if God really sees what you're doing?	Yes	No
Do you find yourself preoccupied with externals?	Yes	No
Has human opinion become more important than God's opinion?	Yes	No
Does your will invalidate the authority of God's Word?	Yes	No
Do you tolerate, even cultivate, evil in your life?	Yes	No
Have you been in a weakened spiritual condition for a while?	Yes	No

If this questionnaire looks bleak, remember, the Lord came to heal the sick—not the healthy. It was for sinners that He came—not for the righteous. Won't you come to Him and give Him your heart? Regardless of how corrupt it is, He can make it clean (Ps. 51:10a). Regardless of how dry and hardened, He can make it warm and responsive (51:12).

 Living Insights

The Corinthians had a case of heart trouble that prompted Paul to send them two detailed letters. Having looked at Paul's second letter, we've found that we have much in common with the Corinthians. As you reflect on your study of 2 Corinthians 8–13, use this time to apply what you've learned to the condition of your heart.

- Review the questionnaire you answered at the end of the lesson above. First, give a diagnosis of your spiritual condition; then, based on the truths you have learned from 2 Corinthians, write yourself a prescription that will put you on the road to optimum spiritual recovery.

My Spiritual Condition

Diagnosis: _____

_____

_____

Prescription: _____

_____

_____

_____

_____

_____

_____

_____

_____

_____

 ***Living Insights***   STUDY TWO

As is our custom when we conclude a series, let's review what we've learned. Look back over your Bible and study guide and record below one significant application from each lesson.

A Minister Everyone Would Respect

Making Good Sense with Our Dollars _____

_____

_____

Fanning the Financial Fire _____

_____

_____

The Trip to Bountiful Giving _____

_____

_____

Giving by Grace _____

_____

_____

A Bloodless Battle Nobody Notices _____

_____

_____

Stabilized Though Criticized _____

_____

_____

Not All "Ministries" Are Ministries _____

_____

_____

The Flip Side of "Fantastic" _____

_____

_____

Gloves of Grace for Handling Thorns _____

_____

_____

Honesty Wrapped in Humility _____

_____

_____

Threads for Mending Frayed Feelings _____

_____

_____

Passing the Faith Test _____

_____

_____

A Love Letter, Sealed with a Kiss _____

_____

_____

Heart Trouble _____

_____

_____

2 Corinthians: A Man and His Ministry

Writer: Paul
Date: A.D. 54–55
Style: Personal, Bold, Defensive

Uniqueness: It is almost impossible to analyze this letter. It seems to be the least systematic of Paul's writing—almost like a journal. These are the words of a man who freely expresses his feelings about himself and his ministry.

Introduction and Salutation	Crucial Concerns Suffering and God's Sufficiency Ministry and Our Involvement Godliness and Its Impact	Grace Giving Example of Macedonians Command to Corinthians	Apostolic Authority Reply to Critics Justification of Ministry False Teachers Visions, Revelations, Credentials, Warnings	Conclusion and Farewell
1:1–2	1:3–7:16	8:1–9:15	10:1–13:10	13:11–14
Scope:	Past	Present	Future	
Issues:	Misunderstandings, Concerns, Explanations	Financial Project	Vindication of Paul's Ministry	
Tone:	Forgiving, Grateful, Bold	Confident	Defensive, Strong	
Key verses:	"For we do not preach ourselves but Christ Jesus as Lord." (4:5a)	"God loves a cheerful giver." (9:7b)	"I shall not be put to shame." (10:8b)	

BOOKS FOR
PROBING FURTHER

W e have reached the end of our journey through 2 Corinthians. And what a journey it has been! In this latter half of Paul's letter, we have encountered such topics as financial responsibility, spiritual warfare, false ministries, God's sovereignty, pain, relationships, and our need for spiritual self-examination.

We hope that the trek has given your spiritual legs a good workout and has shown you some life-changing views along the way. To quench your thirst for some topics we touched on, we are recommending the following books. As you leave Paul and the Corinthians and continue your travels through the Christian life, we hope these books will make the road a little smoother and the journey a little more refreshing.

Bridges, Jerry. *Trusting God*. Colorado Springs, Colo.: NavPress, 1988. Adversity is hard to endure, and even harder to understand. During a time of personal adversity, the author came to know the meaning of God's sovereignty and the deep love He has for His children. What he learned changed his life and will change yours as you realize our Lord's loving control, even when life hurts. Also available is the *Trusting God* study guide for group or personal study.

Gordon, Ruth. *Children of Darkness*. Wheaton, Ill.: Tyndale House Publishers, 1988. This compelling story tells the true-life account of Gordon's experiences with the Children of God cult. She reveals firsthand the deceptive methods this cult uses to lure and keep its members.

Hendricks, Howard G. *Teaching to Change Lives*. Portland, Oreg.: Multnomah Press; Atlanta, Ga.: Walk Thru the Bible Ministries, 1987. One of America's most influential Christian teachers gives seven principles to help you develop a passion for communicating God's Word to all age groups. Whatever your role—pastor, professor, professional, or parent—this book will equip you to teach enthusiastically and effectively.

Hughes, Kent and Barbara. *Liberating Ministry from the Success Syndrome*. Wheaton, Ill.: Tyndale House Publishers, 1987. With broad appeal to pastors and laypeople, this book is for anyone who tends to define success in life by the visible results. Reflecting on their pastoral experiences, the authors encourage churches to view a successful ministry from God's perspective, not the world's.

Lutzer, Erwin W., and John F. DeVries. *Satan's "Evangelistic" Strategy for This New Age.* Wheaton, Ill.: SP Publications, Victor Books, 1989. This book presents a Christian defense against the infiltration of New Age doctrine in the church, home, and political arena. The authors show that because we live in a time of renewed spiritual searching, we have an unprecedented opportunity to share the real gospel.

McDowell, Josh, and Don Stewart. *Handbook of Today's Religions— Understanding the Cults.* San Bernardino, Calif.: Here's Life Publishers, 1982. This handbook will broaden your knowledge of twelve major cults and help you discern between cults and Christianity. The authors discuss the doctrine of each cult and provide an annotated bibliography for further study on this subject.

Picirilli, Robert E. *Paul the Apostle.* Chicago, Ill.: Moody Press, 1986. If your appetite has been whetted to know more about Paul, you'll enjoy this detailed work on the apostle and his letters. This is a valuable resource as both a historical textbook and personal study tool, allowing you to see Paul against the backdrop of his culture.

Timmer, John. *God of Weakness.* Grand Rapids, Mich.: Zondervan Publishing House, 1988. Subtitled *How God Works Through the Weak Things of the World,* this book sets forth one of Paul's major themes in 2 Corinthians. Drawing from his wide reading and personal experience, Timmer offers a feast of wisdom, comfort, encouragement, and biblical application.

Wiersbe, Warren W. *The Strategy of Satan.* Wheaton, Ill.: Tyndale House Publishers, 1979. This is a manual of arms for the dedicated Christian who wants to know how to win at spiritual warfare. Centering his material around Satan as the deceiver, destroyer, ruler, and accuser, Wiersbe emphasizes conquering the enemy by obeying God's truth.

Willmer, Wesley K., ed. *Money for Ministries.* Wheaton, Ill.: SP Publications, Victor Books, 1989. Thirty Christian leaders contributed to this substantive guide to Christian stewardship. Chuck Colson says of this book: "I applaud this much-needed work. [It] provides important and timely guidelines for all evangelicals— whether giving or getting funds—to do so in accordance with God's will and His Word."

NOTES

NOTES

NOTES

Insight for Living
Cassette Tapes
A MINISTER EVERYONE
WOULD RESPECT

Confidence in a ministry hinges on respect for the minister. Few people understood this truth better than the apostle Paul. In the latter half of his second letter to the Corinthian Christians, he spells out the crucial importance of ministering in a way that fosters trust. And by using his own life as an example, he gives us more than an unforgettable autobiography—he gives us a model worth emulating.

			U.S.	Canada
MER	CS	Cassette series—includes album cover	$39.50	$50.25
		Individual cassettes—include messages		
		A and B	5.00	6.35

These prices are subject to change without notice.

MER 1-A: *Making Good Sense with Our Dollars*—2 Corinthians 8:1–9
      B: *Fanning the Financial Fire*—2 Corinthians 8:10–24

MER 2-A: *The Trip to Bountiful Giving*—2 Corinthians 9:1–6
      B: *Giving by Grace*—2 Corinthians 9:6–15

MER 3-A: *A Bloodless Battle Nobody Notices*—2 Corinthians 10:1–6
      B: *Stabilized Though Criticized*—2 Corinthians 10:7–18

MER 4-A: *Not All "Ministries" Are Ministries*—
      2 Corinthians 11:1–15
      B: *The Flip Side of "Fantastic"*—2 Corinthians 11:16–33

MER 5-A: *Gloves of Grace for Handling Thorns*—
      2 Corinthians 12:1–10
      B: *Honesty Wrapped in Humility*—2 Corinthians 12:7–18

MER 6-A: *Threads for Mending Frayed Feelings*—
      2 Corinthians 12:19–13:4
      B: *Passing the Faith Test*—2 Corinthians 13:5–10

MER 7-A: *A Love Letter, Sealed with a Kiss*—2 Corinthians 13:11–14
      B: *Heart Trouble**—Isaiah 29:13–16, Matthew 15:1–20

*This message was not a part of the original series but is compatible with it.

How to Order by Mail

Simply mark on the order form whether you want the series or individual tapes. Mail the form with your payment to the appropriate address listed below. We will process your order as promptly as we can.

United States: Mail your order to the Sales Department at Insight for Living, Post Office Box 4444, Fullerton, California 92634. If you wish your order to be shipped first-class for faster delivery, add 10 percent of the total order amount (not including California sales tax). Otherwise, please allow four to six weeks for delivery by fourth-class mail. We accept personal checks, money orders, Visa, and MasterCard in payment for materials. Unfortunately, we are unable to offer invoicing or COD orders.

Canada: Mail your order to Insight for Living Ministries, Post Office Box 2510, Vancouver, British Columbia V6B 3W7. Please add 7 percent of your total order for first-class postage and allow approximately four weeks for delivery. Our listeners in British Columbia must also add a 6 percent sales tax to the total of all tape orders (not including postage). We accept personal checks, money orders, Visa, or MasterCard in payment for materials. Unfortunately, we are unable to offer invoicing or COD orders.

Australia, New Zealand, or Papua New Guinea: Mail your order to Insight for Living, Inc., GPO Box 2823 EE, Melbourne, Victoria 3001, Australia. Please allow six to ten weeks for delivery by surface mail. If you would like your order sent airmail, the delivery time may be reduced. Whether you choose surface or airmail, postage costs must be added to the amount of purchase and included with your order. Please use the chart that follows to determine correct postage. Due to fluctuating currency rates, we can accept only personal checks made payable in U.S. funds, international money orders, Visa, or MasterCard in payment for materials.

Overseas: Other overseas residents should contact our U.S. office. Please allow six to ten weeks for delivery by surface mail. If you would like your order sent airmail, the delivery time may be reduced. Whether you choose surface or airmail, postage costs must be added to the amount of purchase and included with your order. Please use the chart that follows to determine correct postage. Due to fluctuating currency rates, we can accept only personal checks made payable in U.S. funds, international money orders, Visa, or MasterCard in payment for materials.

Type of Postage	Cassettes
Surface	10% of total order
Airmail	25% of total order

For Faster Service, Order by Telephone

To purchase using Visa or MasterCard, you are welcome to use our **toll-free** numbers between the hours of 8:30 A.M. and 4:00 P.M., Pacific time, Monday through Friday. The number to call from anywhere in the United States is **1-800-772-8888.** To order from Canada, call our Vancouver office at **1-800-663-7639.** Vancouver residents should call (604) 272-5811. Telephone orders from overseas are handled through our Sales Department at (714) 870-9161. We are unable to accept collect calls.

Our Guarantee

Our cassettes are guaranteed for ninety days against faulty performance or breakage due to a defect in the tape. For best results, please be sure your tape recorder is in good operating condition and is cleaned regularly.

Note: To cover processing and handling, there is a $10 fee for *any* returned check.

Order Form

MER CS represents the entire *A Minister Everyone Would Respect* series, while MER 1–7 are the individual tapes included in the series.

Series or Tape	Unit Price U.S.	Unit Price Canada	Quantity	Amount
MER CS	$39.50	$50.25		$
MER 1	5.00	6.35		
MER 2	5.00	6.35		
MER 3	5.00	6.35		
MER 4	5.00	6.35		
MER 5	5.00	6.35		
MER 6	5.00	6.35		
MER 7	5.00	6.35		
Subtotal				
Sales tax 6% for orders delivered in California or British Columbia				
Postage 7% in Canada; overseas residents see "How to Order by Mail"				
10% optional first-class shipping and handling U.S. residents only				
Gift to Insight for Living Tax-deductible in the U.S. and Canada				
Total amount due Please do not send cash.				$

If there is a balance: ☐ apply it as a donation   ☐ please refund

Form of payment:

☐ Check or money order made payable to Insight for Living

☐ Credit card (circle one):   Visa   MasterCard

　　Card Number _____ Expiration Date _____

　　Signature _____
　　　　We cannot process your credit card purchase without your signature.

Name _____

Address _____

City _____

State/Province_____ Zip/Postal Code _____

Country _____

Telephone (____) _____ Radio Station ___ ___ ___ ___
　　　　If questions arise concerning your order, we may need to contact you.

Mail this order form to the Sales Department at one of these addresses:
Insight for Living, Post Office Box 4444, Fullerton, CA 92634
Insight for Living Ministries, Post Office Box 2510, Vancouver, BC, Canada V6B 3W7